The Insider's Gu[...]

INVESTING IN SENIOR HOUSING

America's Best Financial Opportunity
...for the Next 25 Years!

Gene Guarino & Jim Guarino

— GREAT AMERICAN MEDIA —

RAL Academy™ is a trademark of Gene Guarino and Senior Housing Investment Partners™ is a trademark of Jim Guarino.

Great American Media, LLC
5543 Edmondson Pike #50
Nashville, TN 37211

Printed in the United States of America

Library of Congress Cataloging-in-Publication Data is available for this title.

ISBN-13:978-1727270327

ISBN-10:1727270320

Supplementary Writing, Research, Proofreading and Editing:
Jess Stonefield / StoneCityPress.com

Cover and Interior Design: Joni McPherson / McPhersonGraphics.com

TABLE OF CONTENTS

DISCLAIMER

All information contained herein is strictly for limited to informational and EDUCATION PURPOSES ONLY AND SHOULD NOT BE CONSTRUED AS LEGAL, TAX OR SPECIFIC INVESTMENT ADVICE. Each person's situation is unique, and you should consult a knowledgeable advisor before making investment, business, tax, investment or financial decisions.

No guarantees, promises, representations or warranties of any kind regarding specific or general benefits, monetary or otherwise, have been or will be made by either RESIDENTIAL ASSISTED LIVING ACADEMY, LLC, SENIOR HOUSING INVESTMENT PARTNERS, LLC, or GREAT AMERICAN MEDIA, LLC AND/OR ASSIGNS, their affiliates or their officers, principals, representatives, agents or employees. RESIDENTIAL ASSISTED LIVING ACADEMY, LLC, SENIOR HOUSING INVESTMENT PARTNERS, LLC, or GREAT AMERICAN MEDIA, LLC, AND/OR ASSIGNS are not responsible for, and shall have no liability for any investment and/or business success of failure, acts and omissions, the appropriateness of the reader's decisions, or the use of or reliance on this information.

Investing in real estate investing and/or business, does contain risk. Entrepreneurs and investors can both make and lose money on any given transaction. Like the stock market, poor decisions may result in the loss of all or part of an individual's working capital. Caution should always be used.

This information is not to be construed as a security offering of any kind. Prior to making any decision to contribute capital, investors must review and execute all private offering documents, including the project prospectus and the Private Placement Memorandum. Access to information about our investment is limited to investors who qualify as accredited investors within the meaning of the Securities Act of 1933, as amended, and Rule 501 of Regulation D promulgated therefrom.

DEDICATION

This book is dedicated to our amazing parents, Marie Guarino (1925-2014) and Eugene Guarino (1922-1994). Together, they provided us the love, the unending support, and the encouragement to dream and to pursue our highest and best.

SECTION I

How and Why

When we first heard about investment opportunities within the senior housing sector, it was all about one thing: business. As business guys, we wanted to know about the money. How much would we make? How long would it take? How much would we need to invest to get the returns we wanted? Little did we know the topic of senior housing would eventually become more—so much more—to both of us.

Our mother, Marie, had invested her entire life in caring for others. She raised five boys and two girls in the 1960s and 1970s, and we still don't know how she survived it. Us boys practiced championship wrestling in her formal "living room," we got Coo Coo after eating entire boxes of Cocoa Puffs (and were still hungry), and we spent Saturday mornings watching *Soul Train* and *The Munsters*. And this was all before we started a rock and roll band that shook the foundation of the house and then give her potential heart attacks by staying out late—the list goes on!!

After raising seven kids, my mom went back to teaching nursing, which she did for another 12 years. Eventually she retired, and she and our father went to Florida for a stint. As life often happens, our dad became seriously ill with several health challenges. Mom did her best to take good care of him over the next seven years until he passed away. Still, mom wasn't over caring for others. After dad passed on, she went to live with her elderly mother and took care of her for the next five years until she passed away at age 103. Our mom then finally "retired" again to a home in Upstate New York and enjoyed her children and grandchildren for the next 15 years.

During the last several years of our mom's life (from 86 to 89), things changed. She started to forget her meds, to eat dinner, or even remember what we'd just been discussing. For the first time in her life, our mom needed others to care for her. This wasn't easy for her to ask for help or to admit that she needed it. She had always been the caregiver; self-sufficient, stoic, and strong. It was now our turn to do what was necessary and what was right. Senior housing was no longer just a business plan. It was a reality.

Not being prepared and not being aware of what to do or where to go, we started investigating options for care. What we found was a world that was unknown to us at the time. There was an entire industry caring for the needs of those that were unable to care for themselves. This was how we truly began to understand the importance of quality housing and care options for the elderly.

Still, as Dorothy said, there was "no place like home." Our mom had lived in a house for 86 years at that point, never in an apartment or a shared services community. Like most older and staunchly independent people, she wanted to remain in her "home" as long as she could.

Moving to an Independent Living/Assisted Living/ Memory Care community was not an attractive option for her at the time. This is when we became aware of the idea of a community of elderly people living together in a house that provided 24/7 support including cooking, cleaning, personal care support, social, and recreational activities—a place where relatives could still come and enjoy coming to "mom and dad's place." Fortunately for our mother and our family, our two sisters and brother in-law were willing and able to care for Mom with the help of in-home health caregivers during the final years of her life.

Now, having had real-life experience with dealing with an aging parent, senior housing investing became of serious interest. I (Gene) began to research the concept of the senior care home or small house environment with 24/7 care for seniors. I began to look closer at the business model of what we now call "residential assisted living" (RAL). At this point in time, I had been investing in real estate in the Phoenix, AZ market. I had discovered that Phoenix (Maricopa County) had the highest number of senior care homes per capita than anywhere in the United States. I proceeded to negotiate a purchase of my first RAL home, which opened up a whole new window of business opportunity that would change my life and the lives of thousands of others around the country.

Having been a well-respected financial and business educator, investors and entrepreneurs from all over America began asking me for my advice in getting into this new and exciting business model. When I was able, I did consult people, but quickly realized I was only one person and I needed a team to help me to help others. My brother Jim and I had worked together, on and off, for over 35 years at that point. We had invested together and been in multiple businesses together over the years. We traveled extensively training thousands of investors and entrepreneurs in investment real estate and business entrepreneurship. We were both teachers at heart (Dad was a gifted college professor and Mom was an excellent nursing instructor). We had been in the teaching "business" at some level since we were teenagers (no kidding, but that's another story). I had already launched what is now named the Residential Assisted Living Academy (RAL Academy). I asked Jim to help me in helping others in this business—I knew he was the right person for the job at just the right time.

The RAL Academy has since trained thousands of entrepreneurs, investors, seasoned business people, people new to businesses, people making career upgrades, people from all walks of life, and most every career field; real estate investors, entrepreneurs, teachers, medical professionals (MDs, NPs, RNs, LPNs, chiropractors, dentists), attorneys, engineers, executives, white collar/blue collar employees, parents wanting to share, and provide opportunities for their kids. You name it, RAL Academy trains them.

Once someone attends the powerful immersion learning event called the "Residential Assisted Living Business Accelerator" which is where we go into all the nuts and bolts of this business by taking students students through a "boot camp" and a bus tour of actual RAL homes. It really helps them make a commitment to either become an active investor in the assisted living business and it teaches them exactly what to be aware of if they decide to become a passive investor in senior housing. This is why we wrote this book. We want to provide you with the "Insider's Guide" to understanding this special opportunity called senior housing.

Thank you for taking the time to read and educate yourself. You, too, have a unique opportunity to positively impact hundreds of lives and we're thankful to be a part of your success.

Do Good AND Do Well!

Gene Guarino and Jim Guarino

CHAPTER 1

Change Creates Opportunity

Savvy investors and entrepreneurs know the secret: *change creates opportunity.*

And the senior housing story is—above all else—a story about change. It's a story that could create enormous financial opportunity for those who are willing to dig deep—understand the evolving needs of our senior demographic—and use their passion to address those needs in creative, fulfilling ways. In choosing this book, you've taken your first step in the process. This truly is the definitive "Insider's Guide" to understanding both the "why" and "what to do about it" when it comes to senior housing investments. We're glad you're reading it. Let's explore this "change" and discover what this means to you.

Long and short, the change is a demographic one. The number of seniors in our country is expected to double to more than *72 million by 2030.*[1] And by 2050? That *number will hit 83 million.*[2] However, the senior housing story isn't just about numbers. It's about understanding how powerful demographics translate into *meaningful*

---

[1] https://www.census.gov/prod/2014pubs/p25-1140.pdf
[2] ibid.

trends and changes in our society, our culture and the economy. As you know, we're living longer, families are working more, and the number of loved ones available to care for our aging population is dropping at a record pace. But the real message here is that this demographic shift is creating both tremendous wants and needs—and *unparalleled opportunity.*

Enter: senior housing.

The Silver Tsunami

There's no doubt you've heard the phrase: "Silver Tsunami." Yes, it's heading toward our shores at a record unstoppable pace, and it's creating a wave of senior-focused financial opportunities—and issues—in its wake. Although the storm technically touched ground in 2010 (the year the first round of Baby Boomers hit retirement age), the bulk of seniors have yet to reach land. *By 2040, the global population of those 65+ will reach 1.3 billion, double what it is today.*[3] In America, those 65+ will hit 25 percent of the population by 2060. The number of people aged 85 and over is projected to grow from 5.9 million (2012) to *8.9 million in 2030.*[4] The Silver Tsunami isn't just a storm—it's a multi-decade, record-busting gale.

Indeed, whether you're a numbers person or not, it's impossible to ignore the implications of this demographic shift. By 2020, the number of *people aged 65+ will outnumber those under the age of five*—for the first time in global history. This isn't just a "graying"—it's an up-ending of the way we've historically operated as a

---

[3] https://www.forbes.com/sites/nextavenue/2016/05/09/how-to-make-money-from-the-global-aging-megatrend/#5b4d6f75a41f

[4] https://www.census.gov/prod/2014pubs/p25-1140.pdf

nation. As such, let's look at a few "operational" metaphors.

The Silver Tsunami isn't just a storm—it's a multi-decade, record-busting gale.

Imagine you're the manager of a national apple farm. Over the years, you've developed an OK system for harvesting the apples. After all, they ripen at varied times. There's always ample supply and demand, and there are always folks willing and able to pick, ship, and sell them. But all of a sudden, you find out the apple-ripening process is changing. Not only will your trees be producing *more apples that ripen all at once*, those apples will be *staying ripe longer*. What's more, you're having a hard time finding enough quality workers to pick them—especially those qualified to manage the new ripening process. On top of that, you're running out of quality places to store all these apples! How do you keep the apples safe and fresh, while not—pardon my pun—*losing the farm?*

Let's take another example. You and a friend decide to go on a hike. Your plan is to climb to the top of a local mountain. You pack your supplies for the day and do a great job divvying them up throughout the journey. In fact, just before hitting the top of the peak, you finish the last of your water. But as you round the bend to the top of the mountain, you realize what you thought was the peak isn't the end of the climb at all. You still have a lot further to go—and no supplies to help you finish out the journey. You're past the point of no return. How do you stay hydrated when you didn't properly plan for the remainder of the climb?

In many ways, this is what's happening in the senior housing sector right now. The way we planned—

managed—prepared to care for seniors in the past simply isn't relevant to today's—and tomorrow's—senior explosion. With life expectancies increasing from a global average of 49 years in 1955 to nearly age 80 (United States!) today. Seniors aren't just growing in numbers. They're changing the demands on modern medicine, modern families, and even retailers and government regulators. After all, seniors don't age in a bubble. They get sick ... exercise ... shop ... vacation ... contribute to the global workforce. And the more there are of them, the more their needs impact society at large.

Research shows America simply isn't ready to deal with the aging crisis (opportunity as we see it). Just like the procrastinators who fail to stock up on emergency supplies before a hurricane, America has found itself relatively unprepared for the force or duration of the Silver Tsunami. We're overlooking the apple orchard, still looking up the mountain, realizing we are unprepared and have a long way to go.

Increased life spans mean increased chronic illnesses. Increased divorce rates and changing family dynamics mean fewer caregivers to support the aging. (In fact, the caregiver ratio is expected to *drop by more than half* by 2050, from 7:1 in 2010 to 3:1).[5] And a tight—and expensive—real estate market, means fewer options for housing our aging, especially in the type of homelike environment they prefer.

---

[5] https://www.aarp.org/home-family/caregiving/info-08-2013/the-aging-of-the-baby-boom-and-the-growing-care-gap-AARP-ppi-ltc.html

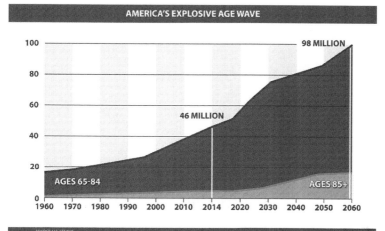

America certainly isn't alone in the aging storm. But in a country like the United States, which focuses so much on independence and technology—we're definitely facing an uphill battle. Not only do we have the fastest growing population of those 60+ (nearly *11 percent*[6] compared to China at 7 percent), our culture is—well—not the most senior-friendly. While some cultures revere their elders, America is known for worshipping the fountain of youth. Which means our aging will need even greater support, beyond their family network, as they get older. Case(s) in point:

- Recent studies showed Americans 65+ were the *only population segment*[7] in the country to experience a significant increase in the number of individuals in poverty, and by 2050, there could be up to *25 million*[8] poor seniors.

6 http://www.visualcapitalist.com/demographic-timebomb-rapidly-aging-population/

7 http://www.businessinsider.com/americans-65-and-up-slipping-into-poverty-2017-9

8 https://www.theatlantic.com/business/archive/2015/12/elderly-poverty-america/422235/

- In an AARP commissioned national survey, *over one-third*[9] of respondents indicated they were lonely. What's more, loneliness was also a significant indicator of poor health, and could lead to other chronic conditions, including increased mortality rates.

- In a 2017 study, Commonwealth Fund's 20th *International Health Policy survey*[10] compared the health experiences of aging adults, including those with high medical needs, in 11 countries (including Canada, Germany, Sweden, and the United Kingdom). The United States ranked either at or near the bottom in multiple categories, including affordability, access, care coordination, and timeliness of care.

- In the same report, researchers showed that overall, 1 in 8 respondents had three or more chronic conditions. In the U.S., that number was *1 in 3*.[11]

- On average, Americans spend *$8,233 per year*[12] on healthcare—some two-and-a-half times more than most other developed nations.

- That's a lot of "not so happy" news for today's aging Americans—but we're believers

---

9 https://www.aarp.org/research/topics/life/info-2014/loneliness_2010.html

10 https://www.commonwealthfund.org/publications/journal-article/2017/nov/older-americans-were-sicker-and-faced-more-financial-barriers?redirect_source=/publications/in-the-literature/2017/nov/older-americans-sicker-and-faced-more-financial-barriers-to-care

11 https://healthjournalism.org/blog/2017/11/u-s-ranks-worse-in-elder-care-vs-other-wealthy-nations/

12 https://www.pbs.org/newshour/health/health-costs-how-the-us-compares-with-other-countries

that *with every challenge . . . there is also an opportunity.* In fact, many sharp investors are beginning to recognize the tremendous opportunity that is the "business of aging."

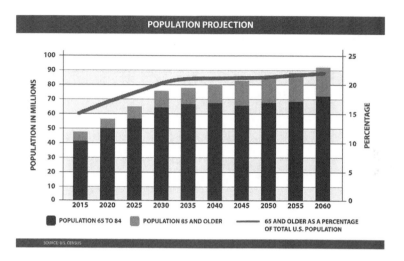

POPULATION PROJECTION

POPULATION 65 TO 84   POPULATION 85 AND OLDER   65 AND OLDER AS A PERCENTAGE OF TOTAL U.S. POPULATION

SOURCE: U.S. CENSUS

The Business of Aging

Capitalism is one of the hallmarks of American culture. And that's a good thing, especially when we realize the Business of Aging may be what shifts our country's focus back where it needs to be—on our aging community. When it comes to the Business of Aging, there are, in our view, two main shifts to consider. The first? It's simply about recognizing the sheer financial power of this growing segment of the population. A growing number of Boomers means retailers will need to focus on different styles of clothes . . . different types of packaging . . . different types of distribution . . . and different types of store layouts directed at Boomer buyers. Indeed, we as a society may not be used to catering to "older Americans," but research shows:

- U.S. consumers 55+ *spend twice as much*[13] as Millennials do

- Half of the U.S. population is over age 50—and they *account for about half of all consumer*[14] spending

- Baby Boomers like to buy—they *spend the most*[15] in all product segments

- Baby Boomers want a variety of options to choose from

- Baby Boomers control some *70 percent of disposable income*[16] in America

- Boomers also account for *80 percent*[17] of all cash currently in savings and loan

By the end of this decade, the spending power of consumers aged 60 and older will hit *$15 trillion globally*[18], up from $8 trillion in 2010. Long story short, *seniors have money, and smart investors will need to cater to what seniors want in terms of lifestyle and comfort if they want to cash in.* That means developing things like aging-focused apps, mobile healthcare, connected devices developed for the Internet of Things (IoT)—*and quality senior housing options*—that promise to make the lives of seniors easier, safer, and healthier all around.

---

[13] https://www.forbes.com/sites/nextavenue/2016/05/09/how-to-make-money-from-the-global-aging-megatrend/#5b4d6f75a41f

[14] https://www.immersionactive.com/resources/24-stats-marketers-need-to-know-about-baby-boomers-in-2017/

[15] ibid.

[16] ibid.

[17] ibid.

[18] https://www.forbes.com/sites/nextavenue/2016/05/09/how-to-make-money-from-the-global-aging-megatrend/#5b4d6f75a41f

The second shift, quite honestly, is more of a movement. Known by many as **Aging 2.0**, it's about recognizing the way that we as a society have traditionally perceived the "senior market" (separate, institutional, fragile) and moving toward a more inclusive idea of aging that focuses on senior wellness, lifestyle, technology, community, and partnership. For instance, in healthcare, we don't just need more caregivers to support our aging. We need *more passionate* geriatric and end-of-life care specialists (in a time when the number of geriatric caregivers is actually declining). In government, we need greater representation from aging Americans who can use their voices in support of healthcare, affordable housing, and inclusion. In the workforce, we need more companies willing to step up to support aging workers, and to take a stand against age discrimination.

Seniors have money, and smart investors will need to cater to what seniors want in terms of lifestyle and comfort if they want to cash in.

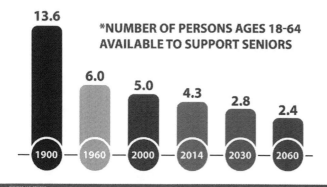

SENIOR SUPPORT RATIO IN DECLINE

13.6

***NUMBER OF PERSONS AGES 18-64 AVAILABLE TO SUPPORT SENIORS**

6.0

5.0

4.3

2.8

2.4

1900 — 1960 — 2000 — 2014 — 2030 — 2060

SOURCE: U.S. CENSUS

And why does Aging 2.0 matter when it comes to senior housing specifically? Senior housing is a unique segment of commercial and residential real estate that doesn't just provide a service—*it changes lives*. And for our investments in aging to be successful, it's imperative that they *change those lives for the better*. That means investing in senior housing projects that support diversity, affordability, comfort, mental health care, and overall social well-being. And as we'll see later in this book, those types of communities, in today's marketplace, are hard to come by. The good news is . . . there are solutions on the horizon ready to be developed and brought to market by visionary entrepreneurs and investors.

CHAPTER 2

Extraordinary Upside Potential

Although senior housing is currently a small yet specialized segment of commercial real estate (CRE), it has grown to become a full-fledged $400 billion industry in its own right, with growth expected to continue *for not just years but decades.* Senior housing investment projects can cost anywhere from $500,000 for an RAL senior care home (with net income streams of $3,000–$15,000 or more per resident per month), to a $500 million multi-story, multi-facility complex. Yes, investors are becoming very interested in this investment sector.

Recession Resistant

But perhaps the most intriguing thing about senior housing is that it is also considered to be one of the most stable alternative investments because it tends to be *recession resistant.* Senior housing has the potential to stabilize your portfolio while keeping it safe as well. In other words, it has a proven track record of weathering the down times. So, now that you know why and how the wave of seniors is creating a demand for housing and what types of housing are available in today's market, let's explore the fundamentals that make senior housing an excellent investment. We'll begin by considering and comparing the many types of investments available in today's marketplace.

Understanding "Alternative" Investments

When it comes to investments, we often think of stocks, bonds, or currency. But there are also what are called "alternative" investments, such as private placement offerings, private equity, venture capital hedge funds, real estate investment trusts, and commodities, as well as other hard assets such as precious metals, rare coins, wine, and art.

Senior housing has the potential to stabilize your portfolio while keeping it safe as well.

Alternative investments are not better or worse than other investment types; they are simply a different classification. All investments carry risk, vulnerabilities, and a potential for growth and cash flow. Diversifying a portfolio with investments that carry different risk and return is an important thing to do when considering your portfolio mix.

Some alternative investments have higher potential returns—and in some cases higher risk than traditional investment opportunities. Uncovering new opportunities within a generally stable asset class, such as real estate, can prove to be a smart move, especially in times of instability.

The Yale Endowment gained fame—and fortune—by focusing heavily on alternative investments in *the past 20 years*.[19] In those two decades, it's experienced an average annualized return of more than 12 percent,

[19] https://news.yale.edu/2017/10/10/investment-return-113-brings-yale-endowment-value-272-billion

compared to the average returns of other college and university endowments at just 7.3 percent. It also outperformed both domestic stocks (7.5 percent) and domestic bonds (5.2 percent) in the same period. Because it falls into the segment of investing known as commercial real estate, senior housing is also considered an alternative investment.

Commercial Real Estate

We want to take a minute to delve a bit further into commercial real estate. Knowing senior housing is classified as part of the commercial real estate sector, it can be easy to assume all segments of commercial real estate deliver the same types of solid, recession-based returns. In fact, however, the opposite is true. While senior housing has managed to detangle itself from the erratic ups and downs of the global marketplace, most other segments of commercial real estate (CRE) have not been so lucky.

When tracked over a ten-year period, senior housing has *consistently outperformed all other CRE segments*, including retail, office space, hospitality, and even apartments. Yes, despite America's housing shortage, even apartments have not fared as well. This is an important distinction. Research from the Harvard Joint Center for Housing Studies and Enterprise Community Partners suggests the number of renters in the United States will increase by four million in the next ten years. Certainly, that presents a need-based crisis in shared housing and apartments. Yet in the past year, returns on senior housing have surpassed those in apartments at a rate of *12+ percent to 6+ percent*[20]—double! The

---

[20] https://www.nic.org/blog/seniors-housing-annual-total-investment-returns-equal-12-79-in-q1-2018/

Silver Tsunami is the reason why.

In fact, historically, only one other sector—the industrial sector—has outperformed senior housing on one- and three-year returns. And even so, senior housing has outperformed apartments, retail, and office space in the same time period.

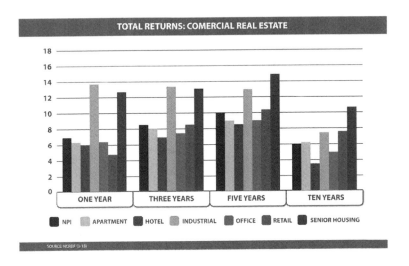

Need vs. Want

In times of economic uncertainty, it is smart to un-yoke oneself from traditional market fluctuations. Senior housing, especially in terms of assisted living and memory care, are necessities. *They're needs, not wants.* And in times of economic uncertainty, those are the kinds of investments that show the most promise, stability, and safety.

Generally speaking, families are less likely to cut back services for an elderly parent than they are to cut back on consumer spending on non-essentials. And if the resident him or herself is funding their senior housing stay, they are likely too far settled to change course just to save a few dollars. This results in a comparatively higher occupancy rate in this sector than alternative real estate asset classes such as retail or hotels.[21]

Families are less likely to cut back services for an elderly parent than they are to cut back on consumer spending on non-essentials.

As we mentioned in the last chapter, this is precisely why assisted living communities continued to *experience positive rent growth* when all other sectors of commercial real estate declined during the recent 2007–2009 recession.[22] And it is exactly why senior housing remains one of the most stable alternative investments you'll find in today's marketplace.

What we're saying here is that senior housing isn't just a trendy blip on the CRE radar. It's a segment that has outperformed for more than a decade and promises to continue for at least two decades more. That's the kind of investment we all need in terms of building security and certainty in an otherwise unstable economic environment.

So, why are we concerned about economic recession and downturn? Because recessions are inevitable. Historically, America has seen recessions every seven to ten years lasting 18-24 months on average. That's why it's never been more important to focus on investments that will fare well in times of plenty and times of uncertainty.

[21] https://www.cbre.us/-/media/cbre/countryunitedstates/media/files/services/senior-housing/shmi-q12018.pdf

[22] http://www.aew.com/pdf/AEWResearchSeniorsHousingInvestment OpportunityMay2015.pdf

Are we trying to scare you? No. We're wanting you to understand why we consider senior housing to be a once-in-a-lifetime opportunity! Never has there been a financial opportunity to invest in a sector with such *historically proven potential*, with demographics that show it will continue to grow for decades to come.

Assisted living communities continued to *experience positive rent growth* when all other sectors of commercial real estate declined during the recent 2007–2009 recession.

Occupancy

Not everything about senior housing is sunshine and rainbows. We in no way intend to represent the market that way. Any investment—traditional or alternative—comes with a degree of risk. Right now, in the senior housing market, that risk focuses on dipping occupancy levels and over-saturation in some markets. Notice we use the term "some markets." Although the market overall has dipped to just under 88 percent occupancy[23] in Q2 2018 (its lowest level since Q1 2010), we are not worried because we know without doubt, the senior surge "age wave" is coming.

Here's why:

1. Anytime new construction comes onto the market—as it has in recent years with senior housing—you'll experience a dip as demand and supply find their balance.

2. As noted previously, we are just at the tip of the Silver Tsunami age-wave. The influx of seniors

---

[23] https://www.nic.org/news-press/seniors-housing-occupancy-rate-drops-below-88-in-second-quarter/

won't just continue over the next two decades—it will dramatically increase. Thus, demand will continue to grow.

3. Also, as will be noted in Chapter 3, the average age of senior housing communities in the United States is well over 17 years old. As new, better, higher-quality communities become available, we'll see that the drops in occupancy aren't in the new-build communities—they're in the lower, less enticing ones.

4. New concepts in service and care will continue to provide and attract people to different options, in terms of care.

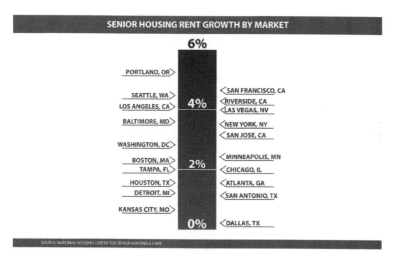

SENIOR HOUSING RENT GROWTH BY MARKET

SOURCE: NATIONAL HOUSING CENTER FOR SENIOR HOUSING & CARE

As with any real estate investment, location is always a major consideration. As noted in the chart below, some markets, such as Dallas, Texas, saw barely any *asking rent growth in Q2 2018*[24], while others, such as Portland,

24 https://info.nic.org/hubfs/NIC_MAP/Data%20Release/2Q18%20Data%
20 Release%20Webinar/ABRIDGED%202Q18%20Webinar%20071818.
pdf?t=1532868952947

Oregon, saw nearly six percent. Point being: every deal and every market is unique. There is still plenty of growth to be found in senior housing in just about every metropolitan statistical area (MSA) throughout the United States.

America's population has grown by 192 million people since 1965, a 70% increase in just over 50 years, to a current population of 326 million. If America continues to grow at this rate, you can expect an additional growth of 228 million people for a population of 550+ million. This equates to almost three times the population in 1965.

So, hold on to your hat! There's lots of room for investors and entrepreneurs wanting to ride this wave!

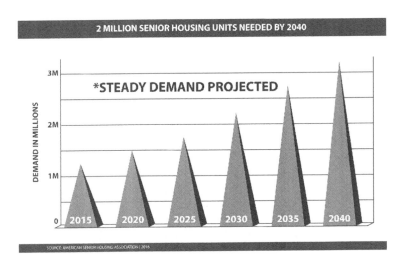

CHAPTER 3

Senior Housing Business Models #1

When you first mention "senior housing," or "group home for the elderly," some people cringe. Their immediate thought is a poorly run old folks' home, where the air smells, people are not properly attended to, and the surroundings are cold and depressing. But the truth is, the range of housing options available to seniors in *today's market* is a veritable smorgasbord of sizes, services, price points, and healthcare assistance. There are options for active, newly retired seniors, seniors with memory issues, and seniors who need 24/7 medical support. There are big-box options (large, multi-storied, institutional-style housing options), *Golden Girls*-style shared-space apartment options, clusters of single-family residential home developments, or individual, single-family homes quietly tucked away inside residential neighborhoods, depending on one's preferences for feeling social and "at home." There's even a high-end senior community inspired by Jimmy Buffett's called Latitude Margaritaville! This is not your mama's senior housing market!

From an investor standpoint, you should understand that senior housing is part of the overall commercial real estate (CRE) market—and it's creating its own unique, high-growth segment. Part healthcare, part hospitality, senior housing is continuing to evolve far past the age-old idea of dark and antiquated state-run nursing homes. As an investor, it's an exceptional time to find—or create—your own niche in this growing marketplace. Indeed, the senior housing market of today is made up of several different product types, each providing specific services and real estate related features. Each investment carries its own risks and rewards. As a senior housing asset class investor, it's necessary to understand the numerous segments and business models within the sector itself.

When it comes to senior housing, there is no such thing as "one size fits all." This will only increase as the Baby Boomers graduate into needing alternative housing and care for themselves. While the WWII generation—those who have most recently used senior housing services—grew up with few choices and lower expectations, today's Baby Boomers are the total opposite. That means the investment environment isn't just about the availability of an elder care building. It's about providing the services Baby Boomers want and need. This an important distinction: both residents and families want, need, and expect a variety of options to choose from when it comes to senior housing. The more you as an investor can differentiate yourself to meet those needs, the more profitable you will be.

Again, change creates opportunity!

I can hear you now: *"Senior housing? How exciting could*

it be?" Let's get your creative juices flowing and help you realize both the potential for change and your own place for participating, as either a passive or active investor.

Change and opportunity are caused by many factors: technology, innovation, societal attitudes and values, politics, interest rates, war, global interconnectivity to name a few.. You may be old enough to remember having a black and white TV, rabbit-ear antennas, and "all three" channels. Or, you may remember when America's

The more you as an investor can differentiate yourself to meet those needs, the more profitable you will be.

shopping experience shifted from walking up and down Main Street USA to driving to the department store, and then from driving to the regional shopping mall to e-commerce and having packages delivered to our front door. Do you remember when Cyber Monday wasn't even a thing?!

How about this: do you remember the "taxi-cab?" What about your first cell phone (50 cents per minute)? How about that place called the "video store," which was replaced by Redbox and eventually, Netflix? Things are shifting and changing rapidly. On top of this, society is learning to adapt and change at a quicker pace. We expect it, we anticipate it, and . . . we embrace it much more easily than we have in the past. That same type of shift is happening in senior housing *right now*, and the sector is ripe with—you guessed it—opportunity!

Research shows America needs to build about two million more senior housing units by 2040 to fill the anticipated need.[25] In case you haven't counted to two million recently, that's equal to housing the entire city of Houston, Texas, give or take a few hundred thousand! It's the equivalent of Sacramento, Tucson, and

Research shows America needs to build about two million more senior housing units by 2040 to fill the anticipated need.

Austin, combined! Every resident in need of not just a bed, but healthcare, joy, and personal attention. That's where the opportunity in senior housing really comes in.

Studies show about *2/3 of existing senior housing properties are more than 17 years old, and about 1/3 are more than 25 years old!*[26] They're antiquated facilities with little room for creature comforts, high-end amenities, or personal attention. We truly believe there's something in senior housing for every investor, whether they prefer ground-up developments or quality-infusing value-adds. Aging Americans—which all of us will eventually be—want better.

As we discussed with Aging 2.0 in the last chapter, the concept of "aging" is changing. And that means catering to the varied—and valid—personal preferences of a growing demographic of seniors. Thus, understanding the senior housing market

*Studies show about **2/3** of existing senior housing properties are more than 17 years old, and about 1/3 are more than 25 years old!*

---

25 https://seniorhousingnews.com/2016/06/09/1-8-million-seniors-housing-units-needed-2040/

26 https://seniorhousingnews.com/2018/07/25/shortage-quality-operators-deterring-potential-senior-housing-investors/

isn't just about understanding how many seniors will need housing in the next 20–30 years; it's about understanding which segment of the market may be most profitable based on today's trends and how those trends may move or shift in the future.

Housing Types/Assistance Levels/Cost and Payment Sources

When spoken of as an investment opportunity, senior housing is often lumped into one segment of commercial real estate. But the fact is, there are a multitude of different types of senior housing options available, based on one's overall level of services needed, financial ability, and personal preferences. Understanding the market means getting a solid grasp of what types of senior housing are available, the difference between the levels of service, and the related financial aspects.

The Insider's Guide will define these important features below.

Levels of Assistance

One of the most common ways we classify the senior housing sector is by levels of assistance. Not all seniors are created equal! A wealthy and active 74-year-old doesn't need the same kind of support as a less active 90-year-old with numerous chronic health conditions. Given that the Silver Tsunami is just getting started, it's important to remember that the bulk of seniors (which started to hit retirement age in 2010) won't likely need communities with high levels of assistance until they reach 80+ years of age (the average age of most assisted living community residents.) Point being: to really know the market, we have to understand what levels of service are needed by aging Americans, who

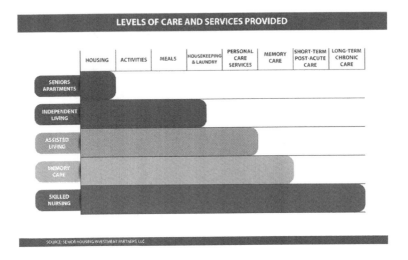

Activities of Daily Living

The acronym "ADL" stands for "activities of daily living." There are five essential ADLs:

1. **Bathing:** personal hygiene and grooming

2. **Dressing:** dressing and undressing

3. **Transferring:** movement and mobility

4. **Toileting:** continence-related tasks including control and hygiene

5. **Eating:** preparing food and feeding

This is important for you, the investor, because you need to have a general understanding of needs of residents as each type of senior housing business model accommodates some level of ADLs—some more than others. When a prospective resident enters a community, for instance, they are generally evaluated by the care team to understand their current and potential future level of care needed. This directly affects the cost of service. Let's review the various terms you'll need to know for evaluating senior housing investment options.

- **Independent Living (IL):** Independent living is just what it sounds like: a community designed for independent seniors who need little to no assistance managing their daily lives. Many independent living, or active senior communities, do still offer services to make their residents' lives easier, such as housekeeping, cooking, transportation, and social engagement. But by and large, residents themselves would be able to manage these activities if they needed to.

Because independent living communities are geared toward seniors who are currently "independent," they are, not surprisingly, the first to enjoy a bump from the Senior Tsunami. On the down side, because independent living is more of a want than a need for active seniors seeking a more laid-back lifestyle, it is more tightly bound to the condition of the real estate market overall. In times of recession, for instance, an active older couple may put off purchasing a home in an active community simply because the move isn't necessary or aren't able to sell their house for maximum value. This, in turn, can impact an investor's returns in this portion of the market.

- **Assisted Living (AL):** Assisted living (AL) communities serve residents with a wide range of health needs. Assisted living communities are regulated and licensed by each state to provide in-house support and services (most states require that services are made available 24/7). This distinction is what helps make AL investments what we call "recession resistant." Because the *services are needed, rather than simply wanted*, they are less tightly bound to the economy overall. In fact, even during the Great Recession, assisted living communities continued to *experience positive rent growth*[27] when all other sectors of commercial real estate declined.

▸ **INSIDER'S NOTE:** *Assisted living support service DOES NOT include medical care. These facilities are not licensed to provide medical services but are permitted to provide medicine management (making medicine available to the resident and keeping accurate records). As such, they are most likely built in proximity to local hospitals and healthcare facilities.*

● **Memory Care (MC):** MC communities provide the same types of care provided in AL communities but with extra support for those dealing with dementia, memory loss, or the related disease of Alzheimer's. What kinds of support? Things like added security, wearable tracking devices, superior caregiver-to-resident ratios, and controlled access—all designed to keep residents safe.

● **Skilled Nursing Facility (SNF), a.k.a. Nursing Home:** Skilled nursing is the most medically intensive segment of senior housing, providing for those who need daily medical care (nursing staff are available 24/7). It's also the least financially stable segment, at this point, due to changes in government funding, as most rely on public assistance. Currently, Medicare pays for only 21-days per related incident of skilled nursing services. After this time period, the Medicare recipient is

---

[27] http://www.aew.com/pdf/AEWResearchSeniorsHousingInvestmentpportunity May2015.pdf

required to pay a portion of the cost. The family needs to determine how SNF's services will be paid alongside their Medicare benefits.

- **Hospice/Palliative Care:** Hospice and palliative care provides end-of-life care for those who are terminally ill. Hospice services are also a Medicare benefit, also with limitations. Some assisted living communities may offer hospice support (permitting there are hospice care services in the facility), while others may offer only hospice care or home-hospice nursing assistance. Hospice care often includes things such as social, spiritual and physical support to help both the resident and their family members.

Both palliative care and hospice care provide comfort. But palliative care can begin at diagnosis and at the same time as treatment. Hospice care begins after treatment of the disease is stopped and when it is clear that the person is not going to survive the illness.

A knowledgeable investor needs to understand the basics of the type of facility/community in which they choose to invest money or time. Let's explore the various business models of each.

CHAPTER 4

Senior Housing Business Models #2

R esearch shows *nearly 90 percent*[28] of those 65+ would prefer to "age in place." At the same time, research also shows some 70 percent of us will need long-term care at some point in our lives. Those who do enter senior-assisted housing—whether they want to or not—generally agree on one thing: *they want to live in a place that feels like home.*

When traveling, some of us like to stay in private, shabby chic Airbnb residences. Others like to stay in top of the line hotels with upscale amenities. Others prefer an RV and others a boat. Preferences don't disappear just because we start aging. That's why there are options for seniors seeking long-term care, and even more room for new niche alternatives to enter the marketplace.

These include:

● **Continuous Care Retirement Community / Life Care Community (CCRC):** Today, most independent living facilities want to accommodate the resident by helping them to "age in place." This is done by making a limited number of resident rooms available for those needing

---

[28] https://www.aarp.org/livable-communities/info-2014/livable-communities-facts-and-figures.html

assisted living services (25 percent on average) and/ or memory care services (15 percent on average). This creates a dynamic whereby the resident can move into the facility while totally independent, and as they require more support services, they can remain in the same facility. The "age-in-place/continuous care" model is well established in today's marketplace. From a business perspective, the concept of aging in place also helps with resident retention, and a recent report[29] from investment firm CBRE shows the model is working. Even when other segments of the senior housing market have experienced dips in occupancy, CCRCs have enjoyed a static *91 percent*[30] national average—not to mention greater rent growth.

The CCRC is an independent living (IL) business model whereby the resident reserves a spot in the community with a sizable entrance fee, typically between $200,000– $700,000. This insures the resident a place in the community with the intention of staying there for the rest of their lives. CCRCs are age-in-place developments with AL and MC on the premises and many also have a SNF on the premise. The entrance fee is retained by the community and returned in part (0-90% depending upon the contract) based on how long the resident had stayed and/or other stipulations in the contract.. While living at the community, there is a monthly fee, based on the level of service the resident requires. On average, this fee would be between $3,000 and $8,000 monthly.

---

[29] https://www.cbre.us/research-and-reports/US-Seniors-Housing-Care-CCRC-Report-June-2018

[30] https://www.cbre.us/research-and-reports/US-Seniors-Housing-Care-CCRC-Report-June-2018

- **Independent, Assisted and Memory Care Living Facility (IL/AL/MC):** IL/AL/MC facilities are typically developed with 50 to 300 beds that are built on several floors resembling the look and feel of a hotel. Most rooms are mini-suites (300 to 600 square feet on average) that include a kitchenette and private bath. There are long hallways, elevators, and a dining room/cafeteria, as compared to the small home environment of walking out of your bedroom and twelve feet to the kitchen of your home.

These are different than the CCRC in that they do not charge up-front large up-front entrance fees, but typically charge a one-time "new resident move-in fee" of between $1,000-$2,500, and then a monthly fee of between $3,000 and $15,000, depending on the location and the level of service the resident needs. Care needs are usually delineated into three levels of care needs. Each level of care results in a higher pricing structure.

IL/AL/MC facilities are designed to accommodate the continuous care feature as discussed above. Some of these facilities may also have an SNF on the premises or close by. Many of these developments come with upscale amenities, including large dining rooms, community rooms, indoor movie theater, library, bar, and local transportation services. IL communities are attractive to the senior who is initially fully independent (still driving and able to care for themselves), who want a community of like-minded people, with all housing needs covered, while having the option to secure the additional care service they may someday need.

SPECTRUM OF CONTINUOUS SENIOR CARE

LOW LEVEL OF CARE	MEDIUM LEVEL OF CARE	HIGH LEVEL OF CARE
HOME CARE NON-MEDICAL		SKILLED NURSING
HOME HEALTHCARE	ASSISTED LIVING	TRANSITIONAL CARE
INDEPENDENT LIVING	MEMORY CARE	SUB-ACUTE
BOARD AND CARE		HOSPITALS

WANT >>> NEED

SOURCE: SENIOR LIVING FUND | 2018

- **Residential Assisted Living Senior Care Home (RAL):**
The upscale, private-pay, small group home environment is quickly becoming the most preferable setting for an elderly person needing 24/7 care. This is done in either a single-family home in a residential neighborhood or a "cluster" of residential-style homes built as a community.

Imagine a beautiful, clean, residential home, in or close to a residential neighborhood, that provides a private bedroom (many with private baths) in a small community of 8–16 people. The small home environment provides the best care ratio available (care ratio is typically five to one, caregiver to resident), cleaning, cooking, medication management, and help with personal needs, including toileting and bathing. A well-run home also provides an enjoyable social environment where families can visit their loved one and enjoy "Mom's and/or Dad's Place."

See **RALAcademy.com** for more information on RAL investment strategies.

- **Cluster Home Senior Care Developments:** Savvy investors are discovering the economic scalability of building multiple residential assisted living homes in one geographic development. One of the newest designs in senior care home design, cluster home developments have shared amenities such as green space, pond, walking trails, beauty salon, and common sitting areas. Building multiple homes on one site allows the investor to create economic efficiencies resulting in increased net cash flow.

Senior care cluster home developments are combining IL, AL, and MC all on one site, thus creating a continuous care model for the resident and family. Imagine four 12-bed AL homes, two 12-bed MC homes, and multiple IL townhomes, villas, and cottages.

See **SeniorHousingInvestmentPartners.com** for more information on cluster home investing.

- **Shared Common Space Independent Living Apartments/Townhomes/Villas/Cottages:** You may or may not remember the 1980's show called the "Golden Girls." It was a TV comedy of four women in their seventies who lived together in a shared home/shared common area arrangement. They are fully independent, with no need for assistance with daily living but value the convenience of an all-inclusive, one-fee living arrangement that covers all expenses, including taxes, utilities, lawn care, and repairs. Each resident would have a private bedroom, and some have a private bath. The common areas would all be shared. This is also proving to be a potentially strong investment opportunity in terms of cash flow.

- **Social/Cultural Shared Housing:** Whether a person needs help with ADLs or is looking for a community of like-minded people, there is a growing opportunity to provide specialized housing for people of common experience, either socially or culturally, such as RAL homes focused on serving Jews, Christians, Muslims, East Indians, Koreans, Chinese, hippies, veterans, LGBT, etc. Other niche opportunities include specialized housing and services for people with physical handicaps, people with autism, those with Parkinson's or MS, and other disabilities, those in post-drug rehab, or those re-establishing themselves after time in prison.

Just as there are all types of seniors, there are all types of people with special needs who need housing. We believe there is already tremendous need and opportunity for this concept, and there will a significant increase in demand for the next 25 years for the smart, forward-thinking investor.

Affordability and Payment

Once a family member has reached the point of needing continuous 24/7 care and attention, assuming the immediate family is unable to provide the necessary level of care, it often becomes a choice between 24/7 private home health care service or a more cost effective and socially stimulating shared-home environment. The question is: *how will the family pay for it?*

Home healthcare agencies charge, on average, between $25–$28 per hour for a skilled caregiver to care for a person in the elderly person's home. Doing the math ($25 x 24 hours per day x 30 days per month), the family would spend some $18,000 per month for 24/7 in-home care at that rate. The family could hire an independent live-in caregiver for about $200 per day, which would still equate to $6,000 per month. Either way you cut it, it's expensive.

That's where senior housing comes in. Many find that it offers a less expensive alternative than in-home care, but that doesn't mean it's "cheap." In fact, one of the most important issues in senior housing today is the issue of affordability. That's why each of the types of housing above can also be divided into segments of price-point and payment type.

Private-Pay vs. Public Assisted Senior Housing

Most high-end, big-box communities and more personalized residential assisted living homes are "private-pay." Private-pay means residents pay out of existing assets, pensions, and/or family member contributions, versus payments from government subsidies such as Medicaid or other public assistance. This could mean using funds from the sale of their family home, funds from a reverse mortgage, or assets such as retirement accounts and savings.

Private-pay homes or facilities can cost up to $15,000 a month in some cases, depending on location and the services offered. The residents and families are responsible for paying the bill, which is not subsidized by any local, state, or federal government.

On the flip-side, there are government subsidized senior care/affordable housing communities designed for seniors. These communities are publicly supported and heavily in demand. Some, especially those in places like New York City and Chicago, have waiting lists years long. Still, because their funding comes from the government, in a time when public funding is in crisis, many consider these types of communities to make less secure investments.

All types of housing have a place in the senior housing market. It is up to each individual investor to find the type that speaks to his or her interests and investment goals.

▶ **INSIDER'S NOTE:** *As a side note, the government-subsidized/public-pay model is not the target investment model we will be discussing throughout this book. We believe that projected cuts in Medicare, Medicaid, and Social Security has the risk of negatively impacting the economic and business model of senior housing in the same manner that government involvement in medicine via managed-care has negatively changed health care services.*

That isn't to say it's a bad investment. There are plenty of projects that are subsidized through various local or state-funded programs such as Medicaid. Just as low-income housing can be a profitable investment if executed properly, so can government-subsidized housing for the elderly. Our primary investment strategy for the purposes of this book, however, is the private-pay

The Insider's Guide focuses on the private-pay business model because of what we see as its tremendous potential for long-term growth and profitability.

business model, where individuals and families use their own resources to care for themselves and/or family members without the political and economic risk of public funding.

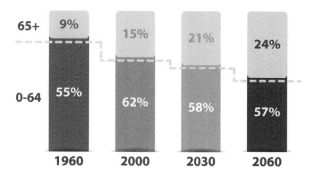

PERCENT OF U.S. POPULATION BY AGE GROUP

PERCENT OF U.S. POPULATION IN SELECTED AGE GROUPS, 1960 TO 2060

SOURCE: U.S. CENSUS

CHAPTER 5

Do Good AND Do Well!

One of our favorite parts about investing in senior housing is the fact that we can "do good and do well." If you've been involved in the investment scene recently, you know the concept of "impact investing," or "socially responsible investing," is spreading. Between 1995 and 2014, the assets under management in the investment class known as "socially responsible investing" (SRI) shot up more than 900 percent[31] according to the Forum for Sustainable and Responsible Investment Foundation. Back then (1995), there were 55 mutual funds focused on SRI. By 2015, there were nearly 500.

In our view, investors have the opportunity to make a huge difference in the lives of seniors by creating a quality, highly-personalized experience in their senior communities. The following are a few examples:

• **Reducing isolation.** Did you know senior isolation is linked to an increase in mortality, dementia,[32] chronic illness, and depression? By creating socially inclusive environments with caring staff, investors can—quite literally—save lives. They can increase quality of life and

---

[31] https://www.cnbc.com/2015/09/24/doing-well-while-doing-good-socially-responsible-investing.html

[32] http://www.aplaceformom.com/blog/10-17-14-facts-about-senior-isolation/

bring true joy to aging Americans during a time of life when many feel abandoned and alone. If that isn't a strong ROI, we don't know what is.

- **Providing greater purpose. Investing in senior housing doesn't just help seniors.** When managed well, it provides meaningful purpose to care workers, as well—and that could be anywhere from a handful of employees to several hundred, depending on the size of the investment community. In managing a small residential community, for instance, you have the chance to build a culture of caring that extends far beyond your care home's walls. It will impact each resident's immediate and extended families, and each caregiver's family, as well.

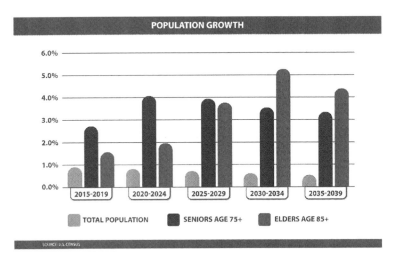

- **Building better business models.** We mentioned times are changing, right? Today's seniors want better care than their predecessors. They want higher-quality services and amenities. They want to be valued for the unique people they are! When you create a residential care home, for instance, you have the chance to build a unique, niche model that fills the gaps where past senior housing models have missed the mark, be it by providing higher quality food, better emotional support, improved family resources, or enhanced connection with the greater community. In doing so, you don't just improve the lives of seniors in your location, you impact the lives of aging Americans all around the country by creating a replicable plan for doing good and doing well.

- **Supporting the local community.** Investing in senior housing helps aging Americans stay in the same communities in which they raised their family, worked, went to school, attended church, and built lifelong relationships. It helps keep them settled, and keeps the community itself working by employing local workers.

- **Focusing on affordability.** Savvy investors who can create a more affordable product than other private-pay senior housing models on the market right now will hit a veritable "bullseye" in the marketplace. You won't just be meeting a segment of high demand, you'll be helping prevent stress among family members and seniors themselves.

How do you know your investment is making a difference? Numbers don't lie. Whether you are investing in a big-box community or launching your own residential community, you have the power to gather analytics and track the progress of your investment on your terms. This could include things like:

Savvy investors who can create a more affordable product than other private-pay senior housing models on the market right now will hit a veritable "bullseye" in the marketplace.

- Improved mood
- Improved levels of fulfillment/life satisfaction
- Decreased mortality rates
- Lower levels of loneliness
- Satisfaction rates among employees
- Satisfaction rates among family members and loved ones

Senior housing is an investment that gives you the power to determine how another human's story will end. You can be the difference between a season of loneliness and isolation, or one of love and dignity.

The Responsibility Risk

Repeat after us: *you do not need to risk your returns to make a difference.* There's a myth, as shared by McKinsey,[33] that investing in senior housing means settling for lower returns than other mainstream, opportunistic investment options. It simply isn't true. We've already illustrated that senior housing returns are historically close to double that of other areas of commercial real estate, including both apartments and retail.[34] The numbers don't lie: *there is a tremendous opportunity to do good AND do well!*

---

[33] https://www.mckinsey.com/industries/private-equity-and-principal-investors/our-insights/a-closer-look-at-impact-investing

[34] https://www.nic.org/blog/seniors-housing-annual-total-investment-returns-equal-12-79-in-q1-2018/

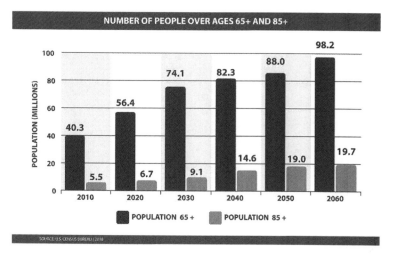

SECTION II

Senior Housing Investment Opportunities

I n the first part of this book, we illustrated the immense investment opportunity in the senior housing space right now. The big question is: would you rather be an "active" investor as an operator/business manager, or would you prefer a hands-off "indirect" approach as a "passive" investor? As with any investment, you'll need to choose what's best for your personal objectives. Your choice will determine your level of responsibility, expertise, time commitment, and ultimately—your ROI.

For instance, studies show passive investments in senior housing, such as private placement offerings, are showing returns as high as 12+ percent over a one-year period. Net profit from even one Residential Assisted Living (RAL) senior care home of 10–16 residents could provide monthly income streams of $10,000–$20,000 or more. Sure, the active investor will put significantly more time and effort into the project. But, he or she will also enjoy greater rewards.

Neither active (direct) or passive (indirect) investing in senior housing is a better investment, but each does suit different investors in different ways, and each comes with its own unique set of benefits challenges. In the next few chapters, we'll go over the ins and outs of each, starting with the benefits.

You can make a "direct" investment and be an "active" investor, or you can "indirectly co-invest" your capital with a team of experts who make the day-to-day management decisions, thereby playing a "passive" role. This would be the case with a private placement offering. As an "indirect co-investor" you are playing a passive role by delegating the management to a team of experts.

Indirect passive investing in this manner allows you to maximize your returns while not taking an active role or investing your time. However, the income classification and treatment of claiming active or passive income is a tax matter. You should consult a knowledgeable tax advisor.

CHAPTER 6

Active Senior Housing Investing

W hen making a direct active investment in senior housing, you'll need more than desire. You'll need knowledge of the industry, specialized knowledge of operations, a strong commitment, a solid vision, enthusiasm, understanding of the local market, marketing know-how, business savvy, people skills, and a genuine love of older people, including patience and empathy in dealing with their families. You'll need a solid business plan and knowledge about the sector—not to mention passion about issues impacting our aging population. After all, as an active investor, you have the chance to impact the lives of individual Americans very deeply, providing care and support at a significant point in their lives. That's not something to be taken lightly! It comes with great responsibility, but also great opportunity in terms of the types of meaningful services you can provide.

Oh . . . we almost forgot . . . it also takes money! It may not be your money, but somebody will need to come up with the financing. The following is our short-list of the types of questions you'll need to answer before getting started. We'll go over each in more detail below.

- How much money will be needed, and how will it be financed? Personal savings? Debt and equity partners? A mix of both? Start-up costs vary greatly, depending which type of community you choose to launch.

- How much time do I want/need to commit? Do I have the capacity to operate more than one unit? Will this be a part-time or full-time venture?

- What is my long-term goal? Do I plan to operate this business for the long haul or sell it once it's up and running?

- How do I select the right location?

- What renovations need to be completed?

- What are the state and local rules and regulations concerning senior housing?

Yes, with an active senior housing investment, you need the willingness to get your hands dirty and think strategically about your own role in the investment. As we can attest, however, you'll also enjoy a tremendous amount of personal fulfillment—and financial gain—in the process.

Let's review the "Seven Steps to Success" in beginning your active investor journey.

Step 1: Select an Investment Type

As you can imagine, your senior housing investment will vary tremendously, whether you are launching a ten-bed RAL senior care home or a 200-bed independent living/assisted living community.

In general, the current national average cost per bed in an IL/AL/MC continuous care community is, on average, $220,000 (varies by location and facility type). Your selection between beginning with one RAL senior care home, a 25–50 bed small facility, or a larger mega-community is a matter of experience and practicality. You may have experience with new construction and development, or perhaps renovating properties. Maybe real estate is new to you, yet you have a strong background in healthcare. Perhaps you are an RN, LPN, MD, or have owned or managed a home-health agency, been a caregiver, a chiropractor or dentist and are looking for a new opportunity. Perhaps you have professional expertise in administrating, managing, or supervising teams, or maybe you're a teacher. Perhaps you've been in various businesses for many years. All these experiences and established skills lend well to owning and operating a senior housing facility or RAL home. Your goal should be to "leverage" your expertise and experience in the best way possible.

Still, when it comes to senior housing, we believe it's best to walk before you run. There are many nuances that you will learn in the process of owning an RAL senior care home, for instance, which can pave the way for doing larger projects in time if you choose. Only you can determine what's best for you but being practical and using good sense is critical in launching any investment. As such, most of our discussion in this chapter will focus on RAL investment.

▶**INSIDER'S NOTE:** *The biggest mistake any investor can make is getting in over their head. That's why we recommend starting with one single RAL senior care* *home, even if you're an experienced entrepreneur, builder, developer, seasoned real estate investor, or healthcare professional.*

Step 2: Decide—Purchase an Existing Business, Renovate, or Build?

As a potential active senior housing investor, you have one of three main choices to consider: 1) purchase an existing/established business, 2) renovate an existing building and start the business from scratch, or 3) launch a new construction development and start the business from scratch. From there, you'll also choose the size of the community, which will range from a small senior care home (6–16 beds, residentially zoned and permitted, and subject to state regulations and local zoning ordinance*) to a large community (60+ beds, commercially zoned and permitted).

Suffice it to say, each of the options above will have a distinct array of details you'll need to dive into to ensure you run a successful, high-quality senior housing enterprise. Most of these details will revolve around real estate and operations/procedures. We'll do our best to outline the main considerations of each here. No matter which option you choose, the secret is playing to your experience and strengths.

1. Buying an existing business (including the real estate)

Buying an existing business is always the simplest and fastest way to get in the senior housing market. Still, a bank or lender will want to put a value on the hard asset (real estate) and a separate value on the business net operating income (NOI/cash flow after expenses but before debt expense) before determining how much it may finance. Thus, if you are buying an existing home/facility, we recommend that you review, at minimum, several years profit and loss for you to determine its true profitability.

Residential real estate and commercial real estate are valued differently, yet, in this case, although the property may be zoned as a residential house, you will be using it for commercial purposes. Our view is that if the real estate is residentially zoned, it needs to be valued based on a hybrid calculation of being a residential (per square foot) value and a commercial (income approach) value, thus combining them and averaging the values.

▶ **INSIDER'S NOTE:** *Once you have the profit and loss in hand, remember to recast the numbers. Recasting is a business management term used to take out any and all owner benefits contained in the financial provided by the current owner. This includes all the deductions taken by the current owner that may or may not transfer to you, such as automobile/travel expenses, food, cell phones, internet/cable, medical, and employee benefits. After recasting, you can get a more accurate* *understanding of what the true cash flow and true expenses would be if you were to take ownership.*

2. Renovating an Existing Structure

There are many details that need to be considered when remodeling a single-family house with the intent of using it for accommodating seniors: flooring types, door sizes, fire suppression systems (sprinklers), auto-locking doors/outdoor fencing (for memory care homes), window size and ease of exit in case of fire, kitchen/family room/dining room openness (for ease of resident care), size of closet space, bathroom functionality, power generators, even furniture types, colors, sounds (music), and monitoring systems. All of these are important, and all cost money.

When purchasing and renovating an existing structure to be used for senior housing, time is always the issue. It can easily take six months to get things done, depending on your level of experience, availability of people to do the work, and your ability to hold people accountable to timelines. All have a major effect on one thing—putting money back in your pocket!

Suppose you have calculated that once your home is filled, you will be generating $40,000 per month gross cash flow. This means that for every 30 days your project is not completed, you are, in effect, losing $40,000 of revenue (which could potentially calculate to $10k–$15k net profit each month when 100% leveraged). Also keep in mind, you will need to consistently validate and budget three distinct flows of capital:

1. Purchase money

2. Renovation money

3. Operating capital until net positive

In that sense, a renovation project is a bit more of a balancing act than purchasing a turn-key community.

> **INSIDER'S NOTE:** *In our experience, even experienced architects need to be informed of the necessary accommodations that make for a well-designed residential assisted living home. That's because they're used to designing "facilities" rather than "homes." When it comes to creating a successful RAL, these details are important, so don't lose track of them.*

3. New Construction and Development

If you have development and/or building experience, in the long run, new construction may be one of the best options. That's because you can design it to suit your scale, which allows you the

> option of making it a larger, more desirable target for acquisition down the road. New construction development is much more complex with multiple additional phases.

As we said earlier on in the book, seniors today want options. They want an experience that feels like home—personalized for their joy and comfort. This brings a wealth of niche opportunities for the savvy investor. Indeed, even if you don't see the type of home you're envisioning on the chart above, that doesn't mean there isn't a place for it in today's market. Here are a few other niche opportunities that hold tremendous potential:

● **Memory Care (MC):** Without question, the small house RAL environment is the most desirable option for people needing a safe, calm, quiet, secure place to live. This is especially true for those suffering with dementia. Dementia is the classification for memory loss illnesses such as Alzheimer's. Individuals suffering from memory loss need a familiar and simple environment, few distractions and less stimulation which can confuse them and cause anxiety. They also need a physically safe and secure environment where they can't easily wander out of sight of a caregiver specially trained in memory care.

Homes/facilities specifically designed for memory care can generate significantly more revenue per bed than an assisted living home/facility. For the additional level of care and attention an individual will need, there will need to be properly trained staff to accommodate this unique challenge of caring for those with memory loss.

Payroll expense will increase approximately 15-25 percent to pay for the higher level of training necessary, but in most cases, bottom line revenue will increase by about 50 percent, making MC a serious consideration when thinking through which business model you will undertake.

Homes/facilities specifically designed for memory care can generate significantly more revenue per bed than an assisted living home/facility.

As mentioned earlier, combining MC services in the same community as IL and AL is a common concept and a well-proven business model.

Visit **RALAcademy.com** for more information on memory care.

- **Cluster Senior Care Home Development:** The "cluster home" concept is one of the most exciting concepts in Senior Housing, combining the "continuous care" concept by providing IL/AL and MC with the multiple RAL senior care homes all on one parcel. This concept provides the investor tremendous scalability of resources while providing families the comfort of knowing their loved one will have the additional care provided as the need arises without moving to another location.

Currently, most of these offerings do not require the resident to pay a large upfront fee of hundreds of thousands of dollars as with a CCRC. The cluster home concept provides residents with a small community (10-16) inside an actual house versus a facility.

You will find clusters of two, four, six, eight, ten homes on one parcel and some with IL villas/cottages as part of the overall development. It is common to use several of the houses for assisted living support and several for memory care support.

Visit **SeniorHousingInvestmentPartners.com** for more information on passive investment opportunities of this type.

● **Shared Common Space Independent Living Apartments/Townhomes/Villas/Cottages:** See Chapter 2

● **Housing Based on Shared Interests/Values/Culture:** See Chapter 2

Step 3: Develop a Financial Plan

One of the first questions most investors have about starting their own senior care community is this: how will I finance it? Every situation is different, but each will likely include a mix of debt (secured loans), private equity (secured and unsecured), and/or seller financing (short-term or long-term).

What's needed is a financial plan including a "pro-forma," which is a projection of future performance. The financial plan will document the following:

1. **Project Data**
    Project data will include the constants you use for the overall financial analysis, including number of beds, projected revenue per bed, inflation rate, vacancy rate, caregiver ratio (day and night), hourly wages, and start-up month (if a start-up), to name a few.

2. **Budget/Costs**
    This includes the cost for the real estate

and/or business, new construction costs or renovations needed, soft costs (engineering, architect, market/feasibility study, legal, licensing, permitting), financial, and closing costs.

3. **Financing Analysis**
   This calculates the cost of debt service (loans from banks and/or preferred debt payments to investors).

4. **Operating Expenses**
   Management fees, payroll, fixed and variable operating expenses.

5. **Cash Flow**
   Monthly and annual cash flow analysis for ten years.

6. **Appraisal (Current and Future Value)**
   It will be necessary to estimate a current fair market value (FMV) and a potential future value based on using well accepted valuation standards. This will be used for determining a loan-to-value (LTV) percentage used by lenders as well as the potential return-on-investment (ROI) for equity investors.

Step 4: Site Selection

Yes, there's a lot to consider when determining where to make a potential investment. Choosing the right site for a senior housing project is based on many factors:

- Federal and state regulations
- Local zoning code, population density

- Demographics/growth/income
- Competition
- Highest and best use of the real estate
- Neighborhood (if it's a residential assisted senior care home), including potential NIMBY issues (see below)*
- Accessibility

That's why research, including strong and up-to-date market research, is so important. Yes, there may be a great need, but you still need to follow state regulations and local zoning code. Every state has its own set of rules for licensing care facilities. Every local municipality has zoning codes and restrictions thereof, some more lenient than others.

In most cities, the presence of assisted living communities is fairly common. But when it comes to building in residential neighborhoods, acceptance and familiarity varies greatly from state to state.*

▶ **INSIDER'S NOTE:** *Focus on an area of town that has strong income demographics to appeal to families that can afford private-pay rates.*

Arizona is on the leading edge, having been one of the early adopters of permitting residential homes to be used for assisted living services. Maricopa County (Phoenix proper, approximately 4.2 million people), for instance, has over 2,800 licensed facilities since first launching the model 30 years ago. California, Oregon, Colorado, Texas, and Florida have all followed suit, yet to a lesser degree. The entire state of Florida, with a population of

21 million, only has 3,000 +/- licensed facilities. On the opposite end of the spectrum, Rhode Island just opened its first residential assisted living senior care home in 2017. The entire state of Tennessee has many large IL/AL/MC communities but less than ten quality RAL senior care homes as of this writing. Clearly, there is plenty of opportunity in the residential assisted living industry!

Step 5: Operations

All well-run businesses have established systems, operations, and procedures (SOPs) that are documented, reviewed, and adhered to. In the business of senior housing, a policies and procedures document is required by state law, in most cases. This document details every aspect of every detail that happens within the home/facility. Whether it be how medications are stored, how medication is made available, how disbursement is documented, how menus are made available for all to see, how many fire alarms are required, what procedures to follow in case of emergency, how to handle a resident in case of a fall—*everything*. Most states have specific requirements that must be followed and included in the state-specific P&Ps.

These can be drafted by a professional or purchased from specialists. At RAL Academy, we provide an entire set of policies & procedures for our advanced-level clients.

In most cases, large facilities sub-out the management functions of the senior housing community to a third-party. All systems, operation, and procedures, including staffing and all employee-related details would be the responsibility of the management company. Normal management fees would be between 5-7 percent of the gross income. In the case of RALs, you are the business manager who hires the team to oversee and manage your operation. This would include potentially hiring a supervisor, who oversees the house manager, who oversees the caregivers.

▶ **INSIDER'S NOTE:** *We recommend establishing your own "management company" separate from the entity that owns the real estate. This will minimize your liability exposure. In effect, you "rent" your facility to the management company that you own and control.*

Step 6: Staffing/Human Resources

An important aspect of operations is hiring and staffing the best possible team for your home or facility. This brings up the issue of resident-to-caregiver ratio. The best ratio available for elderly is in the RAL-style senior care home. Well-run homes provide a care ratio of 5:1. That's one certified caregiver for every five residents. This is far superior to larger facilities, that in some cases run well into the 15:1 care ratio or higher.

Imagine needing assistance going to the bathroom and needing to wait 15–20 minutes for a caregiver to answer your call—and then another 15–20 minutes to get the help you need back to your chair when you are finished. This is not uncommon in many assisted living facilities, and this is not an exaggeration. Several experienced caregivers who have worked at larger facilities have told us how discouraging it is to work at an understaffed facility knowing the residents aren't being properly cared for.

Those who are directly providing care in the home or facility are the most important link in terms of overall success. A skilled, loving, and certified caregiver is the key to a well-run operation. They are the ones who the resident and their family most interact with—not the owner/operator (who may only show up once every few weeks). Caregivers report to a house manager, and the house manager would report to you, the business manager (owner/operator), unless you hire a supervisor to oversee several houses.

Finding and retaining quality, dependable caregivers who can speak English well is one of the challenges of operating a well-run senior care home or facility. It's important to note that caregivers, although highly skilled and loving people, are not highly paid. Most work 12-hour shifts, three to six days a week and are paid an average of about $10–12/hour.[35] In fact, wages for nursing assistants, home health aides, and personal care aides have actually gone down[36] in the past ten years. As the owner, you will want to think of ways to recruit and retain the best caregivers for your community.

We want to reiterate: your staff is onsite 24/7 keeping residents safe and secure. You are not there personally providing care for residents.

Those who are directly providing care in the home or facility are the most important link in terms of overall success. A skilled, loving, and certified caregiver is the key to a well-run operation.

[35] https://thediwire.com/guest-contributor-recruitment-strategy-important-factor-senior-housing-investment/

[36] https://www.disabilityscoop.com/2017/05/09/severe-shortage-care-crisis/23679/

You will find mom and pop operations where the owner is also a 24/7 caregiver. This is a huge cause of burnout and not the kind of model that will bring peace and prosperity to your life. In a well-run RAL, you'll typically have a mix of care providers and administrative providers to help you keep the ship moving forward.

Administrator

Most states require a licensed administrator to be listed for each home/facility. Each state regulates the administrator's level of engagement, documented experience, and how many house/facilities they can oversee. The owner/operator will, in some cases, elect to be the administrator. This typically takes between 24–100 hours of education requirements (some live and some online), testing, and formal certification by the state, and in some states, several years of hands-on experience is required. Many owner/operators will choose to hire an administrator who might be supervising and overseeing operations of multiple houses.

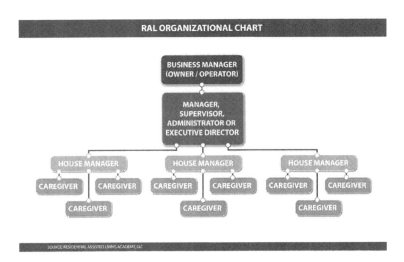

Step 7: Marketing

All success in business is a result of great marketing. You can have the best service, the best care ratio available, and the best value, but people still need to know you exist and what's in it for them. That's what all marketing boils down to.

- **Senior Care Placement Agents:** Placement agents are a primary source of getting new residents—but they can be expensive. Also known as leasing agents, they are in the business of working with families, helping educate them on their options and then getting the family member placed in the most suitable environment. You may have heard of the company called Place for Mom. This is the most well-known placement source in America. Place for Mom is a data collection web-portal. Once you log in, your name and information is given to local placement agents who then contact you to introduce themselves and their services. Placement agents charge the home/facility a placement fee of 50%–125% of one month's resident fee for every placed resident. Not all placement agents are affiliated with Place for Mom. Private agencies typically charge less than a Place for Mom and the fee is paid over a 60-day period.

Placement agents charge the home/facility a placement fee of 50%– 125% of one month's resident fee for every placed resident.

- **Referral Sources:** The best source of new residents is through effective referral marketing. This starts by keeping a database of everyone in the community who is involved with servicing the elderly community: geriatric doctors' offices, durable medical equipment supply companies, home-health agencies, care-coordinators, discharge departments and social workers at local hospitals and skilled nursing facilities, and receptionists at local churches and synagogues. These are people that need to know about what you have to offer.

Establishing face-to-face relationships with these people is important, so they can put a face to a name. We recommend creating an email database and sending them updates of interesting information happening at your home or facility, helping them become more aware and keeping you in mind for when the time is right. Even competitive IL/AL/MC communities should be viewed as a potential two-way referral source. There will be times when someone who tours their facility finds it is not the right fit for them, and the same goes for you. There will be times that either your pricing or availability doesn't fit the needs of the family, and you'll need to refer them to someone. It's best when it goes both ways.

• **Website/Social Media:** A professional looking and operating website is a must. Again, think in terms of daughter Judy. Mom falls for a second time in Austin, Texas, where Judy grew up and mom still lives. Judy lives in St. Louis, MO. Mom ends up in the hospital for three nights, Judy takes vacation time to fly in to see her. The hospital discharges her to the skilled nursing facility for rehabilitation (Medicare typically only pays for 21 days, then the individual becomes partially responsible for the costs involved). The SNF let's Judy know that Mom is not going to be able to go home without having 24/7 support. Judy needs to be home on Monday for work. She gets on the internet and searches for solutions. Mom is determined to stay in Austin as long as she can. Your website becomes the vehicle of introduction for you to secure a simple phone interview to determine if Judy's mom is a potential candidate for your home or facility.

If so, you immediately set an appointment to have them come over and meet the house manager, the caregivers, and some of the other residents. The website is not there to provide all the information they need; it's there to give them just enough of an experience to cause them to give you a call to learn more, and so you can set a time to have them over. Once they are there, they will get a feeling as to whether or not this is a good fit.

▶ **INSIDER'S NOTE:** *Assisted living senior housing is an event-driven business. People typically don't get on waiting lists unless it's a CCRC or perhaps an IL facility. People only make the move to an assisted living facility once they are no longer able to properly care for themselves at home.*

Daughter Judy will also look for reviews of previous families' experiences. Understanding how this targeted profile (women and men ages 45–65) use the internet for research will show you how you best need to reach them. For example, today the highest segment of Facebook users is women ages 45–60. That should tell you something; your home or facility needs a Facebook page with a community of followers that leave their comments (hopefully good ones!).

▸ **INSIDER'S NOTE:** *As an owner/operator, it's important to remember who your real customer/ client is going to be. More often than not, it will be the son or daughter of the elderly parent—and in this case, more often the daughter. Yes, mom or dad will make their desires known, but it's often the children's responsibility to get things taken care of. As such, put yourself in "Judy's" shoes. She is between 45–65 years old, still busy as can be, possibly working full-time and possibly still caring for kids and/or grandchildren. Meanwhile, she's doing her best to care for an aging parent who now has needs that are much like a child's.*

Judy may be energy- and time-strapped, emotionally drained, stressed, and worried. So, when we say the place needs to be "accessible," I think you can understand why. Imagine having worked all day, wanting to get home to relax and take your shoes off, but also wanting to visit with your mom or dad—30 minutes away on the other side of town. Even the thought is exhausting! Combine that with the fact that visiting itself often takes a lot of emotional energy, depending upon the parent's condition. Imagine if mom or dad doesn't recognize you from time-to-time— or at all. That's painful. So, remember, Judy is your client/customer, and you want to make life as enjoyable and as easy as possible for her whenever possible. That's why having your home or facility in a populated, easily accessible area is very, very important.

▶ **INSIDER'S NOTE:** *You may find that many communities, especially those where residential senior care has not yet developed as fully, need to be educated and informed of the needs of the aging population. You may even find a "NIMBY" issue (a.k.a. an outcry of "Not in my backyard!") and other resistance, especially when opening a residential housing operation.*

The federal government has addressed the issue several times since 1968 with the Fair Housing Act, as well as the 1988 Fair Housing Act Amendment, both of which prevent discrimination. Familiarize yourself well with these laws to ensure a successful project.

Visit **RALAcademy.com/FHAA** *for a copy of the 1988 FHAA.*

Understanding and Managing Risk

As in any entrepreneurial endeavor, there is risk involved. Some people are more risk tolerant than others, and not everyone is geared for entrepreneurial work. We'll address this in the final chapter. Most importantly, if you are going to take on this business venture, be sure to get the best training and best advice from the best source possible. It's always in your best interest to carefully count the costs of doing business and understand as much as possible before you begin. The alternatives are costly mistakes of time, energy, and money.

CHAPTER 7

Active Investing Benefits

Just as a parent loves all his/her children equally, we like to say we like both active and passive senior housing the same. That said, we love them differently. They each have different strengths and weaknesses, and we can get along with each one a bit better depending on what's happening in our life at that time. The following are the strengths of each. It's up to you to decide which one is best for you based on how much time and money you wish to invest, how you're hoping to diversify your portfolio, and your personal tax strategy, skillset, and passion points.

Here are some benefits of owning and operating a senior home/facility as an investment:

1. Control

You maintain complete control of the vision and implementation of the project. There is no one perfect way to design, develop, and then operate a home or facility.

2. Income

Most of us invest for two primary benefits: income (cash flow) and growth (capital appreciation). Some of us want one more than the other, and some want both. But the bottom line is we all need a solid *return on investment (ROI)* for an investment to make sense. As mentioned above, an active investor not only invests money, but also lots of time, physical and emotional energy, and hard-earned knowledge. As such, their rewards tend to reflect additional benefits as well as cash flow and appreciation.

To understand how powerful the cash flow potential is in senior housing, let's look at a comparative example:

As an active investor, suppose you were to invest in and hold 50 single-family houses with an average fair market value of $250,000 ($12,500,000 portfolio). As any smart investor, you do your best to leverage the investment with debt and use as little out of pocket as possible. The net result is $10,000 per month positive cash flow, after factoring in debt service (or a reasonable return on your own capital invested) and out-of-pocket expenses/maintenance. Not a bad idea. Over time, the mortgages get paid off. Meanwhile, you enjoy the tax benefits, real estate appreciation (if any), and . . . the maintenance. I can see you shaking your head, imagining the toilets, tenants, and turnover involved with managing 50 rentals! It's a solid financial return (especially if leveraged using other people's money), but a lot of work—and headaches—in return.

As another example, suppose you decide to invest in a typical franchise. First, in most cases, you may need to be "accredited", which means you must have a verifiable net worth of one million dollars, excluding your primary residence, or you must be able to show that you've earned a minimum of $200,000 for each of the past two years (and you expect to do so again this year). Next, you will need to have between $175,000-$250,000 (in most cases) in liquid reserve capital ready to invest for carrying costs and wages until the franchise becomes profitable. Then, you also need to qualify and personally sign for a large bank loan to build out the establishment, which will typically put you in debt for three to five years. All this to earn a pre-tax income of $60,000! Yes, the average retail franchise owner takes home just about $60,000 before taxes.[37] Turns out, you'd need to own multiple units to start living the high life.

Now, suppose you choose to own and operate one single family house ($500,000) and convert it to a RAL residential assisted living senior care home ($100,000 renovation, plus $75,000 in carrying costs). You'll hire a house manager who follows your systems operations manual, including all policies and procedures, takes all calls 24/7, and reports to you only when absolutely necessary. You net the same $10,000 per month and you're working only five to ten hours a week (once your systems and residents are in place). Plus, when owning and operating an assisted living senior care home, you help the local community by providing a needed service, and you gain tremendous satisfaction and fulfillment. Which active investment would you rather manage . . . 50 rental houses, a few franchise locations, or just one RAL senior care home?!

▶ **INSIDER'S NOTE:** *There are few business ventures that have such strong and predictable upside potential as does this **proven business model** of RAL senior care homes. Small RAL homes have*

37 https://www.cnbc.com/2016/05/11/the-hard-truth-about-franchise-business-profitability.html

been ignored by the larger players in this asset class because owning and operating RAL homes is not viable for a large company. This leaves a tremendous opportunity for the small business entrepreneur/investor.

3. Growth (Capital Appreciation/Equity)

Real wealth is not the income you earn, it what you keep in the long run.

A well-managed, well-run RAL senior care home that has a few years of documented financial records can potentially sell for a multiple of two to five times the net earnings on top of the value of the underlying real estate which may have also appreciated. For the example above:

Real Estate Value:	**$600,000**
RAL Business Value:	$120,000 *(annual net earnings)*
	X 3 *(estimated earning multiple)*
	$360,000
TOTAL RAL Market Value:	**$960,000**

Once your RAL home is "stabilized," having reached full occupancy for over a year at maximum resident rates, you have created a business asset potentially worth hundreds of thousands of dollars—even if the real estate has lost value. The business value is based on the income generated from the business which pays "rent" to you to lease the real estate, which at the same time stabilizes the value of the real estate.

Now, imagine participating in one of the newest and most powerful investment strategies, a senior "cluster home development," where you build two to ten senior care homes and independent living villas/cottages on the same location. More on this concept later.

5. Real Estate and Business Tax Benefits

You know by now that real estate ownership and business are the two most proven vehicles for building wealth in America. Both are favored by tax law. With senior housing, you combine both and get the best of both . . . enough said!

6. Sellable

If well-maintained and prof-itable, senior housing assets are highly sought-after in-vestments. They are relatively liquid in comparison to other forms of commercial real es-tate and businesses. Many

Once your RAL home is "stabilized," having reached full occupancy for over a year at maximum resident rates, you have created a business asset potentially worth hundreds of thousands of dollars.

people want to get in on this business, and if and when you decide to sell your operation, there are plenty of potential buyers ready and waiting. The lower barrier of entry and the lower price point make for an attractive opportunity for more potential buyers.

▶ **INSIDER'S NOTE:** *In the example above, suppose you'd like to sell your business for its maximum value. You could offer it for sale at $1.1 million and require the buyer to secure their own funding, however, many potential buyers would have to walk. On the* other hand, if you listed the same opportunity for $1.2 million and offer to "owner finance" with $200,000 down, your phones will likely ring very quickly.

Many people want to get in on this business, and if and when you decide to sell your operation, there are plenty of potential buyers ready and waiting.

There are many people interested in purchasing a functioning small business who don't have the ability to finance a start-up or may not be bankable at that level. The best part: in this example, instead of paying a large capital gains tax, you'd receive a monthly income for the next three to five years, at which time the new owners should be able to qualify for bank financing to pay you back. During this time, you could lease the property to the new owner, giving them the option to buy. You would also file a UCC-1 filing on public record securing your interest in the business and its assets in case of default. This is the type of powerful financial strategy we teach at the Academy's events in Phoenix.

Visit **RALAcademy.com**.

7. Leverage

Most business start-ups are not easily bankable. Banks invest in assets they understand and are familiar with. They prefer business ventures that have provable current income. Let's face it, they aren't in the business of taking much risk. Banks understand real estate and real estate values, putting you in a position of being potentially unbankable as compared to most other business ventures. In the example above, a business that has several years of substantive financials is much more bankable.

8. Tax Benefits

The tax code is written to the benefit and favor of small business and real estate ownership. There are tremendous tax benefits to owning any type of real estate. Suffice it to say, as an active owner/operator, you would receive the standard business deductions as you would in any business, including employee salaries, equipment, utilities, etc. But you also receive the depreciation deduction related to ownership of real estate. The Tax Cuts and Jobs Act (TCJA) of 2017 significantly changed, mostly to your benefit, the tax advantages of owning real estate. And, if you establish the real estate and management company in separate entities, you may gain even greater protection from taxation. Make sure your tax advisor is knowledgeable in tax strategy, entity formation, and asset protection.

9. Investment Capital Availability

Money needs to be put to work. In fact, if money isn't working, it's losing value. It's not easy to deploy money in safe, secure, and strategic opportunities. It takes time and work to find good ones. Here's the point: people are looking for good investment opportunities.

They need intelligent, hardworking, visionary entrepreneurs who have great projects to invest in. People understand the need for specialized housing for the elderly, many times because they have had the experience of dealing with a parent or relative in their later years. The lure of senior housing investment goes deeper than just "show me the money." Many investors like to be involved with opportunities that are meaningful, interesting to them, and in their local area.

10. Unlimited Income Potential

Being in this business, your income potential has no ceiling. You can buy, build, or manage as many locations as you choose. It's all a matter of the time and effort you want to put in. There are no territory restrictions as with franchising, the market will continue to expand over the next 25 years, people will continue to live longer, and Baby Boomers will want comfort and choices.

Again, passive investing in senior housing has a tremendous future. Learning how to identify quality deals will pay off, time and time again.

11. Time Freedom

People wonder if it's really true that you can set up two, three, or four RAL senior care homes using the same supervisor to oversee the individual house managers, and still only work five to ten hours per week. Well, yes, it's true! That's exactly what I (Gene) have done. There are times that I don't go to the senior care home but once every six weeks. Yes, there will be times that attention will be needed, but the secret is to have clearly documented business systems and policies and procedures as well as a solid supervisor and care teams overseeing the residents. Keep in mind, there will be an intensive investment of time and energy on the front-end, yet it has the potential to pay you for years to come once systems are in place.

12. Personal Use

Owning your own RAL senior care home is a great way for people to be ready in case they ever need assistance with their own daily living. No one wants to have to leave their own home, but the reality is, many of us live long enough to get to the place where we do need assistance cooking, cleaning, and caring for ourselves. Chances are, we'll all be involved in assisted senior housing one way or another—we'll either own it ourselves, or we'll pay someone else to live in theirs!

Owning homes/facilities is an excellent means of also providing for other family members when in need. Putting a loved one in an assisted living setting is stressful and costly for many families. Having the ability to have your own place ready to go is wise and cost effective.

13. Personal Fulfillment

As previously mentioned, we teach all our students to, "Do good and do well!" This is a business where you have an opportunity to positively impact hundreds of people's lives, even with just one home, and at the same time, earn a highly respectable income, enjoy the tax benefits, and build significant wealth . . . all at the same time!

As you can see, there are tremendous benefits to being an active senior housing investor. The personal satisfaction goes beyond the incredible income streams and equity growth.

SECTOR DESIRABILITY

ACCORDING TO THE ULI 2018 EMERGING TRENDS IN REAL ESTATE, SENIOR HOUSING RANKS FIRST AMONG SEVEN RESIDENTIAL PROPERTY TYPES IN 2018 FOR BEST INVESTMENT AND DEVELOPMENT PROSPECTS. NEARLY 30% OF SURVEY RESPONDENTS RANKED INDEPENDENT AND ASSISTED LIVING FACILITIES AS AN EXTREMELY FAVORABLE INVESTMENT.

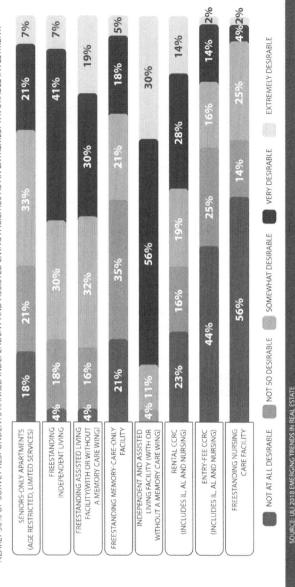

	NOT AT ALL DESIRABLE	NOT SO DESIRABLE	SOMEWHAT DESIRABLE	VERY DESIRABLE	EXTREMELY DESIRABLE
SENIORS-ONLY APARTMENTS (AGE RESTRICTED, LIMITED SERVICES)		18%	21%	33%	21%	7%
FREESTANDING INDEPENDENT LIVING	4%	18%	30%	41%	7%
FREESTANDING ASSISTED LIVING FACILITY (WITH OR WITHOUT A MEMORY CARE WING)	4%	16%	32%	30%	19%
FREESTANDING MEMORY-CARE-ONLY FACILITY	21%	35%	21%	18%	5%
INDEPENDENT AND ASSISTED LIVING FACILITY (WITH OR WITHOUT A MEMORY CARE WING)	4%	11%	56%	30%	
RENTAL CCRC (INCLUDES IL, AL AND NURSING)	23%	16%	19%	28%	14%
ENTRY-FEE CCRC (INCLUDES IL, AL AND NURSING)	44%	25%	16%	14%	2%
FREESTANDING NURSING CARE FACILITY	56%	25%	14%	4%	2%

SOURCE: ULI 2018 EMERGING TRENDS IN REAL ESTATE

CHAPTER 8

Passive Senior Housing Investing

I f your head is spinning, don't worry! As we shared in Chapter 5, active senior housing investment is ripe with reward. Still, not everyone is ready or willing to commit to such a large venture, especially when just entering the senior housing market. You may love the promise of senior housing investing—but you aren't all that interested in doing the necessary work of being an active investor. It's OK. You can still benefit from the huge opportunity available in the senior housing sector—in the form of *passive investing*.

As you might have guessed, passive investing is the chance to earn a promising return-on-investment (ROI) while having *other people*—experts in the senior housing industry—make the hard decisions about where to invest, when, who will manage operations, and in which types of communities. This takes the pressure off of you to learn the ins and outs of the industry, while still allowing you to passively benefit from the Silver Tsunami.

Indeed, although many associate passive investing with things like the S&P 500 or other types of funds that "auto buy" and "auto sell" based on index performance, that definition has grown tremendously. Opportunities such as private placement offerings, crowdfunding, hedge funds, private equity, and REITs all offer an "invest it and forget it"[38] model, allowing investors to enjoy the benefits of venture capital projects, commercial estate investments and other alternative investments without having to invest personal headspace into building them. Indeed, there are a number of different ways to invest passively in senior housing. In this chapter, we'll go over the most popular methods of investing, the benefits and drawbacks of each, and how to go about selecting the most promising opportunity.

The two most popular ways to invest passively in senior housing are through private placement offerings (also considered private equity) and REITs. The following is a brief overview of the private placement offering and the REIT.

Private Placement Offerings (Private Equity)

A private placement offering (or non-public offering) is a securities offering not sold through a public offering such as stocks on the open market, but rather through a private offering, mostly to a small number of investors grouped together.

A private placement offering can also be referred to as a "private placement" or a "syndication." Syndication is the term used for the process of raising the funds for an investment. It's an effective way for investors to pool their resources in projects/properties that are larger than they could afford or manage on their own.

---

[38] https://seekingalpha.com/article/4104433-passive-investments-cre-really-exist

A private placement may be for one specific investment, or the offering may be for a "fund" where the money is "pooled" for investing in multiple projects/properties. These can also be referred to as a "blind fund" where the investor is not sure exactly what assets are being purchased or held in the fund. Whether the investment capital is for one asset or many, projects are selected primarily for the purpose of; retrofit/rehabilitation, a value-add renovation or to enhance revenue by further stabilizing the asset, new construction—or a mix of all three—in a variety of locations.

Your investment capital may be used for secured debt or unsecured equity. This is why and how the term "private equity" is used. Whether or not funds are secured or unsecured, projects are selected by the syndicator or an investment manager. The syndicator typically participates in the offering retaining an equity interest in the project as a general partner, limited partner, managing member or stockholder depending on the type of entity holding the asset. The investment manager may or may not be the syndicator and may receive compensation for overseeing the capital under management.

Private offerings are great for entry level investors because they require little knowledge of the industry. On the other hand, the investors themselves have no say where their dollars are placed (unless your input is requested)—so you better have solid trust in the investment manager and his/her ability to manage your funds well!

▶ **INSIDER'S NOTE:** *Crowdfunding gained popularity in 2013 with the Jumpstart Our Business Startups (JOBS) Act. The act initially allowed primarily accredited investors to gain access to real estate deals via crowdfunding and peer-to-peer lending. The act also provided similar protections to smaller private equity funds as it did to crowdfunding platforms. As of 2015, both equity funds and crowdfunding have the opportunity to open offerings to both accredited and non-accredited investors. The only major difference: private placement offerings generally have a much higher minimum investment. In the crowdfunding sector, investments may start as low as $5,000—compared to $50,000 for a private placement.*

A significant benefit of private offerings—similar to REITs—is that investment managers will generally try to decrease risk for their investors. Unlike REITs, however, private placements are classified as an alternative investment. That means they do not correlate as highly to the stock market and offer a means to diversify one's stock-heavy portfolio. Also on the "up" side: because they are managed privately, private placements/equity funds are generally run more tightly and can respond more quickly to changing market conditions. Whereas REITs may have a lengthy or complicated process for approving investment locations, equity companies can move with greater agility, scooping up great opportunities when and where they present themselves—even beyond primary or secondary markets.

> ▶ **INSIDER'S NOTE:** *An accredited investor is defined as an individual with a net worth (excluding their primary or secondary residence) of $1 million, verifiable income of $200,000 a year for the previous two years (or $300,000 combined with a spouse), or officers and directors of the issuer and various institutions that have more than $5 million in assets.*

Real Estate Investment Trusts (REITs)

While there are both public and private REITs, we're going to focus here on the most common: public REITs. If you're active on the stock market, you may have heard of Community Healthcare Trust (CHCT), Healthcare Trust of America (HTA), or Omega Healthcare Investors (OHI). That's because, like stocks, REITs are traded openly on public exchanges, making investment in senior housing relatively easy for the entry-level investor.

The largest benefit of investing in a healthcare REIT is that you can jump in the market at a lower price-point than any active investment, or any other passive investment opportunity. Whereas a private placement may require a $50,000 minimum, and be open to accredited investors only, for instance, public REITs are typically open to all investors. Whether you've only got a few thousand in savings or even be "non-accredited"—it doesn't matter. What's more, public REITs are also liquid, meaning you can pull your money out easily if you need it. However, as with any stock or mutual fund, there may be a loss in share value or a back-end "exit fee." Many REITs are well diversified, and managed by experts—making them, in our view, the easiest way to jump into the market.

So—if REITs are so easy, why isn't everyone investing in them? First, although senior housing has consistently been the highest performing sector of commercial real estate, healthcare REITs haven't always shared the same success. In fact, REITs have been the weakest performing real estate sector in the past.[39] Why? Keep in mind that a healthcare REIT is just that: a REIT focused on healthcare real estate—not senior housing specifically. That means REIT managers are creating portfolios with a mix of medical office buildings, skilled nursing facilities, and senior housing communities.

While that sounds good from a diversification standpoint, it's important to remember that the demographic surge of seniors does not support all segments of healthcare in the same way. As such, we urge caution when it comes to investing in healthcare REITs. REITs are affected by the volatility of the market. Yes, we are sounding the alarm of the inevitable market correction. Do your legwork. Learn as much as you can about past performance. And learn all you can about the investment strategy of the REIT managers.

Another negative of REITs: they won't necessarily diversify a stock-heavy portfolio. Because they are traded publicly, they won't provide the same level of diversification[40] as, say, investing in commercial real estate directly. So—if you're looking to senior housing to offset the stocks in your portfolio, do some thorough research. It's possible an investment in a healthcare REIT won't have the impact you're intending. Lastly—not to knock them too hard—but there is one more significant

[39] https://seekingalpha.com/article/4159137-healthcare-reits-life-support

[40] https://www.forbes.com/sites/forbesrealestatecouncil/2017/12/28/buying-rental-property-vs-investing-in-a-reit-part-i/#686695bc62ce

negative to REITs that bears mentioning: for tax purposes, dividends are allocated to ordinary income, capital gains, and return of capital. As REITs do not pay taxes at the corporate level, investors are taxed at their individual tax rate for the ordinary income portion of the dividend. And depending on how well your chosen REIT performs, those gains could be significant.

Understanding the Deal

Even though it's a passive investment, it's imperative that you take time to fully understand the parameters of your investment. In some cases, such as REITs, the parameters are fairly simple: you buy and sell when you're ready, and you pay tax on any earnings as you would on earned income. But with other deals, such as private placements, it's a completely different story. Each deal comes with its own unique set of projected returns, distributions, equity participation, and tax implications. We'll do our best to cover the major aspects of most equity deals below.

Show Me the Money

In any deal, the big question is: *when will I get paid?* The truth is, it depends. **Your private placement memorandum (PPM)** will outline various aspects of your deal, including:

- How long your capital will be tied up (generally 2–7 years)

- How much your fund manager will be receiving in fees

- Whether or not your fund manager will receive his or her fees before investors do

STAYING POWER AND INDUSTRY TRENDS

JLL HAS NOTED A NUMBER OF EMERGING TRENDS IN THE SENIORS HOUSING SECTOR, AND TO GET A SENSE OF THE POSSIBLE STAYING POWER OF THESE TREND, THE SURVEY RESPONDENTS WERE ASKED TO EVALUATE THEM.

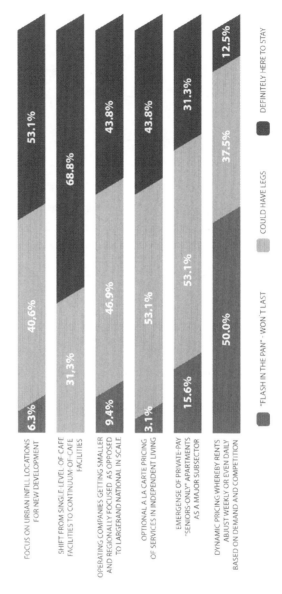

FOCUS ON URBAN INFILL LOCATIONS FOR NEW DEVELOPMENT — 6.3% | 40.6% | 53.1%

SHIFT FROM SINGLE-LEVEL OF CARE FACILITIES TO CONTINUUM-OF-CARE FACILITIES — 31.3% | 68.8%

OPERATING COMPANIES GETTING SMALLER AND REGIONALLY FOCUSED AS OPPOSED TO LARGE AND NATIONAL IN SCALE — 9.4% | 46.9% | 43.8%

OPTIONAL A LA CARTE PRICING OF SERVICES IN INDEPENDENT LIVING — 3.1% | 53.1% | 43.8%

EMERGENSE OF PRIVATE-PAY "SENIORS-ONLY" APARTMENTS AS A MAJOR SUBSECTOR — 15.6% | 53.1% | 31.3%

DYNAMIC PRICING WHEREBY RENTS ADJUST WEEKLY OR EVEN DAILY BASED ON DEMAND AND COMPETITION — 50.0% | 37.5% | 12.5%

"FLASH IN THE PAN" - WON'T LAST   COULD HAVE LEGS   DEFINITELY HERE TO STAY

SOURCE: JLL RESEARCH REPORT | SENIOR HOUSING | INVESTOR SURVEY AND TRENDS | WINTER 2018

- Projected annualized rate of return

- Any other terms specific to your deal

Do not just browse this document. Read it. Redline it. And be prepared to ask hard questions before wiring your money to the bank. For instance, if the PPM states the management fee of your chosen offering is greater than three percent of committed capital, that's a red flag. It would mean, for instance, that a manager of a $50 million fund would make $1.5 million, even if the fund weren't successful! Find a fund that runs lean and mean, and you're more likely to enjoy its success.

▶ **INSIDER'S NOTE:** *A PPM is not a business plan. Its purpose is to provide the investor descriptive but not persuasive content. It should allow the investor to decide on the merits of the investment by presenting the information in a factual, concrete manner. It must address risks, use of funds, company operations and the primary management team behind the operations.*

The PPM will include:
- Introduction
- Summary of Offering Terms
- Risk Factors
- Description of the Company and the Management
- Use of Proceeds
- Description of Securities
- Subscription Procedures
- Exhibits

To see an example of a PPM, visit **SeniorHousing InvestmentPartners.com/PPM**.

Some deals will offer a single method of return-on-investment (ROI), and others may allow the investor to participate is several. The following are the most common forms of ROI:

● **Preferred Returns:** Preferred returns are typically distributed either monthly or quarterly once the project is cash flowing, as in a new construction project. Offerings that provide preferred returns often receive a lower overall return than those providing a share of the profits (profit sharing) and/or equity, but they do enjoy a fairly steady flow of income throughout the deal. Preferred returns are ideal for those who primarily want income during the term of their investment. The term "preferred" indicates that the investor will receive their stated ROI before other parties, most particularly the general or key partners.

● **Profit-Share:** Private offerings that provide preferred returns may also provide the investor the ability to share in profits. However, the investor would not receive those profits until later in the investment life-cycle when the project is—you guessed it—profitable.

A benefit of profit-sharing is that it allows investors to enjoy deductions associated with "passive losses," or the losses incurred at the start of a project before it becomes profitable. While the investment may still be a positive one, the output of capital early in in the deal still makes for great tax savings early on. Discuss this with your CPA or tax attorney.

● **Equity Participation:** In reading the PPM of a private

offering, you will find if you receive any ownership or equity participation in the deal. In many cases, equity is provided to investors along with preferred returns and profit-share. Equity includes the future growth in value (appreciation) of the asset you have equity ownership in.

● **Fixed Income:** A fixed income offering provides a "fixed" return each month to investors. Because it is a lower risk, it is generally a lower return than preferred returns, profit-sharing or equity participation. It is ideal for those seeking set reliable income each month, and who prefer simple tax filing (the earnings are taxed as income).

Understanding and Managing Risk

The question we hear most in passive investing is this: what if the investment tanks? Short answer: As with any investment, you could lose it all. That's part of the risk you take. If it was a senior housing project, the underlying asset would have some value. It would most likely be sold, liens and debts would be satisfied in priority order, if there is anything left, it would distributed back to investors based on their priority rights.

Part of your job as a passive investor is to limit the potential of loss through a solid process of vetting, research, and gut checks.

The truth is, even passive investments require at least some commitment on the part of the investor. After all, it's your responsibility to choose the investment you feel presents the strongest opportunity—with the partners or operators you trust the most. *This responsibility will always lie on your shoulders.* Handing over your money and hoping for the best—it's simply not enough, even in today's senior housing market. Thus, we recommend you make the following steps part of your investor's toolkit before *every investment* you undertake.

- **Do your research.** Not all investment managers, REIT managers, and community operators are created equal. In fact, of all active large cap managers in 2015, over 65 percent[41] performed worse than the S&P 500 over a one-year period. Even worse: That number jumped to 80+ percent at five years. If you tend to "flip for it" when making your investment decisions, you'll likely end up burned. Investors need to take time to do their research on the front end to ensure the company is reputable, trustworthy, and performing in line with their estimated returns.

it's your responsibility to choose the investment you feel presents the strongest opportunity— with the partners or operators you trust the most.

- **Know who you're dealing with.** The greatest indicator of a successful senior housing investment is the history of the operating partner. The entire success of the investment will depend on the ability of the operator to effectively market the offering and manage operations.

- **Prioritize transparency over potential profits.** Always choose deals where communication and transparency are strongly encouraged. Make sure your investment manager is available for questions when you have them— and that he or she won't disappear when your check is signed. Check the LinkedIn profiles of the investor

---

[41] http://www.investopedia.com/advisor-network/questions/how-many-mutual-funds-beat-sp-500-percentage-basis-after-operational-fees/

relations professionals on the team. Verify credentials and confirm that fund updates will be provided on an ongoing basis. Because senior housing is a lucrative segment of CRE, a lot of "newbie" fund managers are jumping on board. Those aren't the opportunities you want to sign onto. Note: Do these things *before* signing on the dotted line. Once you hand over your money: it's too late.

▶ **INSIDER'S NOTE:** *If you can't find evidence of a certain fund on the SEC website, don't panic. Regulation D (Reg D) exempts some companies offering securities from registering with the SEC. The goal of this ruling is to improve access to capital markets for smaller companies that would otherwise be shut out due to the cost of SEC registration. In 2013, the SEC gave even more freedom to Reg D funds, allowing public advertising and solicitation to accredited investors. Long story short: if you can't find your deal with the SEC, talk to your chosen investment manager to see if their deal is a "Reg D" deal."*

● **Know the market basics**—and find a fund manager who knows the rest. Know enough to ask the right questions and find an investment manager who understands that global trends simply aren't applicable in every deal. They can vary by state, market, and even market sub-segment (assisted living vs. skilled nursing, vs. independent living). Relying solely on market trends will always leave you trending downward.

- **Diversify.** An oldie but goody—always keep diversification in mind. No matter how good a deal may seem, it's *no good* if it matches every other deal in your portfolio. Find an investment partner who understands the importance of diversification—for you and the fund itself. If you get any pressure, for instance, to invest more or bigger in a similar deal, back away quickly. No reputable fund manager would risk your financial well-being for the good of the fund.

Every investment comes with a degree of risk. In general, the higher risk, the higher the *potential* reward. We recommend taking time to thoroughly review the PPM or contract agreement for your passive investment thoroughly with a financial professional to ensure you understand those risks completely.

Yes, passive investments require much less elbow grease than active investments, but that doesn't mean you can close your eyes and hope for the best. Do the work. Take it seriously. The more you know, the more successful you will be.

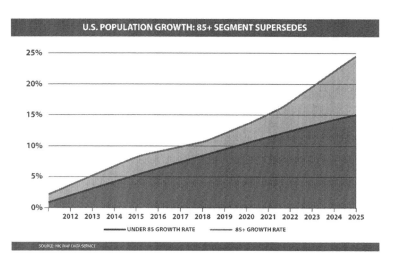

U.S. POPULATION GROWTH: 85+ SEGMENT SUPERSEDES

UNDER 85 GROWTH RATE   85+ GROWTH RATE

SOURCE: NIC MAP DATA SERVICE

CHAPTER 9

Passive Investing Benefits

E ven if you choose not to actively invest in senior housing, you can still benefit from the previous scenarios in many ways. In addition to the majority of the benefits of active direct investing above, below are just a few of our favorite benefits of passive (indirect co-invest) senior housing investing:

1. Requires Limited Knowledge

The greatest benefit of making a passive investing in senior housing is that it allows you to jump into this commercial real estate sector (CRE) sector with incredibly limited knowledge of the industry. Passive investors may average returns of 12 percent or more *(CBRE Senior Housing & Care Market Insight, Q1 2018)* while doing absolutely zero work to keep a community running—or learning the ins-and-outs of successful CRE investment. Fund managers, for instance, will carry the weight of researching things like:

- Gross income: how much cash will be generated in the community

- Expenses: how much will be spent, and how those expenses will be managed

- Profit or loss

- Deal structure: How the deal is structured to mitigate risk, including things like waterfall structures, fixed vs. variable interest rates, debt coverage ratio (DCR), debt service, etc.

- Common issues like slow-moving construction and community politics that could cost the deal profit

- Problems such as heavy payroll and expenses, especially in value-add investments

Indeed, although we generally think of fund managers as simply money movers, they're doing a lot of work behind the scenes to keep their investors' money safe and profitable.

Meanwhile, you as a passive investor sit back and enjoy your earnings, which—depending on the details of your contract—may even come in the form of monthly payments.

2. Diversification and Risk Management

We all know diversification is key to successful investing. But not all diversified portfolios are created equal. Investing in precious metals like gold may do well in periods of economic crisis, but they have remained relatively static over time. As one writer noted, gold's value is based in fear[42]—not potential returns.

And what about equities (i.e. the stock market)? In the past 15 years, the S&P 500 has returned ten percent

---

[42] https://www.forbes.com/sites/johnwasik/2016/11/18/four-reasons-why-gold-is-a-bad-investment/#79e8c2033a03

annually (minus dividends). Sounds OK, right? Research shows,[43] however, if you happened to miss the ten best days in that 15-year investment period—say by moving your investments around—your annual return would instantly drop by half to five percent. And if you missed the 30 best days? You would actually lose money! That means, even though it's technically "liquid," your capital isn't worth much if you don't lock it up for the duration of those 15 years. And that doesn't even get into the issues of volatility that make the market unreliable.

And what about bonds? When interest rates go up, bond values go down. Historically, every one percent increase in interest rates results in approximately a ten percent drop in bond values. The result is a teeter-totter ride of potential volatility—in what's considered to be one of the most stable investments! Meanwhile, take a look at the year-over-year recession-resistant stability in investing in senior housing.

3. Requires No Time Commitment

Unlike an active investment in RAL, which will still require 5–10 hours of oversight per week once the community is stabilized, the job of managing your passive investment is done the moment you sign the contract. What's more, as noted in the example above, senior housing investment won't necessarily require you to invest your money for 15 years to see the same returns as you would in the S&P 500. The industry has outpaced the S&P's ten percent return at one-, three-, five-, and seven-year levels, according to CBRE.

---

[43] https://twocents.lifehacker.com/time-is-your-most-important-investing-asset-1828260510

SENIOR HOUSING RETURNS

	INCOME RETURNS			CAPITAL (APPRECIATION) RETURNS			TOTAL RETURNS		
	TOTAL NPI	TOTAL MULTI-FAMILY	TOTAL STABILIZED SENIOR HOUSING	TOTAL NPI	TOTAL MULTI-FAMILY	TOTAL STABILIZED SENIOR HOUSING	TOTAL NPI	TOTAL MULTI-FAMILY	TOTAL STABILIZED SENIOR HOUSING
1ST QTR 2018	1.12	1.06	1.36	0.58	0.44	0.79	1.70	1.50	2.14
4TH QTR 2017	1.16	1.07	1.34	0.63	0.55	2.79	1.80	1.62	4.12
ONE YEAR	4.66	4.37	5.59	2.38	1.95	6.94	7.12	6.38	12.79
THREE YEAR	4.78	4.54	5.70	3.81	3.34	7.17	8.72	7.99	13.16
FIVE YEAR	5.03	4.72	6.09	4.79	4.12	8.43	10.00	8.99	14.88
TEN YEARS	5.53	5.20	6.61	0.54	1.03	3.73	6.09	6.10	10.52

SOURCE: NCREIF

4. Passive Gains and Losses

Depending on the terms of your passive investment, you may also enjoy significant tax benefits, for example, in the first few years of any new development deal, you may experience passive losses due to the output of capital.

Private placement offerings are an excellent opportunity for your IRA or 401k retirement funds.

Those losses—though not long-term—can potentially be written off to offset other income or gains in your portfolio. Discuss this with your tax advisor.

5. Deferred Taxation

Another way an indirect passive investor can benefit from senior housing investments is via 1031 exchange opportunities. A 1031 exchange allows you to defer taxes on an earnings from one real estate investment that you roll into another qualifying "like kind" investment. Yes, there are specific guidelines that need to be considered, but the ability to indefinitely defer taxes is tremendous.

Private placement offerings are an excellent opportunity for your IRA or 401k retirement funds. If you have an IRA or a 401k from a previous employer, these funds can become "self-directed" and used for private placement offerings.

6. Socially Responsible Investment

You won't be working with seniors every day, but you can still feel good that you're making a positive impact in their lives by making a socially responsible investment! The demographics don't lie. There will soon be a huge lack of quality senior housing available for our aging Americans. By investing now, you can help solve that problem, and ensure better, happier lives for countless people around the country.

Senior housing has consistently outperformed all other real estate asset classes for the past ten years.

There is tremendous opportunity awaiting you as a passive investor in senior housing. Senior housing has consistently outperformed all other real estate asset classes for the past ten years.

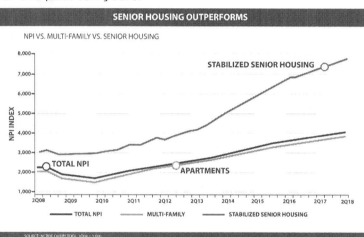

CHAPTER 10

✦

Know Thyself

Over the past 40 years, we have made many types of "investments" of money, time and energy. We've invested in just about everything you can imagine:

- **Real Estate Investments:** residential and commercial (wholesale, fix and flip, renovations, buy and hold)

- **Traditional Investments:** stocks, bonds, precious metals, mutual funds, FOREX, options

- **Alternative Investment:** private placements, tax liens, real estate and business assets backed notes

- **Business Ventures:** tech-based and software development, media (radio, publishing and records), service businesses (financial planning, investment broker, insurance services, food services, recording studios, music school), educational services (advanced training for adults in entrepreneurship, real estate, business, personal/professional development), marketing (digital, affiliate, network, affinity, direct and public seminars), business consulting, professional speaking, book authoring

Oh yes, even collectibles (cars and guitars)!

Some of these "investments" have been very successful and some . . . not at all. However, each investment of time and money has given us more understanding of what makes sense and why. From our experiences, we've learned a lot over the years of what to do . . . and what not to do.

We understand what it's like to face our fears. To be very honest with you, we've not always been "victorious." We've both had major business, financial, and personal setbacks. There have been times we've procrastinated, times we've lacked self-confidence, times we've experienced both self-doubt and defeat. Yet we've chosen not to quit. We've found the passion to learn, grow, and *move forward* every time. This book is a collection of those learnings, and we're so proud to be able to share them with you now.

We've learned first-hand that "winning" in the investment world requires a knowledge of one's own strengths and weaknesses, as well as the market itself. Obviously, these are many reasons we've chosen to plant roots in the senior housing world. What we've shared here doesn't even begin to crack the surface.

We've both had major business, financial, and personal setbacks. There have been times we've procrastinated, times we've lacked self-confidence, times we've experienced both self-doubt and defeat.

If you are going to be an active participant, you'll need to put the shovel to the ground, dig up the dirt, plant the seeds, water and weed, and plan for a harvest based on what you believe is the best decision for you and your family. But active investments aren't for everyone.

That's why we've shared the promising opportunities in passive investments in senior housing, as well. We truly believe there is an opportunity in senior housing for every investor. It's your job to determine which one fits you.

A older and wiser friend of ours once quoted Shakespeare saying, "Know thyself and to thine own self be true." How right he was. Life is a journey of self-discovery. Hopefully the older we are, the wiser we become—and the smarter our investing will be, too!

It's taken us years to "know and be true" to ourselves . . . to realize that money is money, but there is more to life than having a fat bank account. Being able to serve others by doing business with integrity and excellence, using our talents at their highest and best level, trusting that God knows exactly what He is doing having provided us with tremendous opportunities and surrounding us with wonderful people—and enjoying the entire process!—for us, that's what life is about. Yes, we've been blessed!

More than anything, we have two hopes for this book we've shared with you: 1) that we have provided you with the foundational information you need to make an intelligent decision about becoming a senior housing investor, and 2) that we have inspired you to begin imagining the role you can play in supporting our aging Americans in this Silver Tsunami. Let's see if we can help you by answering a few final questions about senior housing investment.

What type of investor are you?

Yes, you can learn to be an entrepreneur and become a successful active investor in senior housing. But, you may need to break-out of your current mindset of being an employee. Not everyone is designed to be able to take the risks that it requires to do business well. If you've been in business before, you know what we mean. If you haven't, you need to think deeply about what you are and aren't willing to sacrifice for success. Perhaps you already know you have what it takes.

Sacrifice

If you want to be a successful active senior housing investor, it will—at least initially—come down to sacrificing a few of life's basics: time, money, comfort. But it also takes self-discipline, vision, commitment and a support network. You may be able to commit the time, discipline, and sacrifice your comforts, but maybe you don't yet have the money or support. That's okay. Every successful person has to start somewhere. The secret is knowing how to get what you don't have—and this takes resourcefulness and personal ambition. You will consistently need to see the glass at least half-full of opportunity. Success in life doesn't go to naysayers—and it doesn't listen to them either. The question is: are you willing to make those sacrifices? If not, a passive investment may be better for you.

Risk Tolerance

You need to know that in the world of investing, every deal comes with a unique risk/reward ratio, and every investor comes with a unique risk/reward threshold. Do you know yours?

Obviously, greater risk generally means greater reward. You aren't going to get a 15 percent ROI putting your money in the bank, are you? But the good thing about senior housing is that it has provided consistent returns for more than a decade. Even those with a lower risk threshold should be able find at least a passive deal that meets their needs.

On the line below, decide where you would put yourself in terms of being willing to risk your capital. "1" means you aren't willing or able to take any risk— in fact, you actually feel uncomfortable leaving your money in a bank, believing there may be a bank run at any time. On the other side, a "10" makes you a "speculator." At this point you are basically a gambler who knows you might, and are willing to, lose ALL your money at any time.

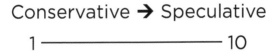

Both types of people do exist, and neither extreme is better than the other. There are people who are willing to throw money at deals hoping they will explode in value, and there are those who never put their money to work for them. The best is to find a healthy medium—a calculated risk based on good information that fits your family's investing needs.

Level of Financial Sophistication

Next, honestly ask yourself, "how knowledgeable am I when it comes to investment management?" Would you consider yourself "non-sophisticated" or "sophisticated?" Remember, the more informed you are, the more you understand the intrinsic and potential value and the potential pitfalls, the better decisions you will make. It is your responsibility to mitigate risk, and that starts with knowing your own limits.

Non-sophisticated → Sophisticated

1 ——————————— 10

Investment Goal

Next up, what do you want this investment to do for you? Do you want or need an income stream? Might you want or need tax benefits? Or, might you prefer the majority of your return in capital gains at some future point in time whereby you can potentially roll the gain into another investment, further putting off the taxable event? All great questions! And both active and passive investments can provide all of these things, if chosen correctly. Your job is to know which goals you want to achieve, and how you plan to make them happen.

For instance, if you're angling toward a passive return but need a stream of income from your investment, look for a deal with a preferred return and maybe a share in the profits. If you don't need regular income, perhaps opt for more equity if its available.

Terms of Investment

How long are you willing and able to keep your money committed? Do you prefer

Your job is to know which goals you want to achieve, and how you plan to make them happen.

to invest in assets you can sell quickly if you need to? Private placements offer a specific "term" for keeping your money invested in the deal. Generally they will be from 2-7 years. The longer your money is committed, (generally) the greater the potential return. A long-term passive investment might work well for someone who doesn't want to be thinking about where to reinvest every couple of years. Keeping money active and working is what investing is really all about. It takes time and work to keep money well deployed. That's why once you find a type of investment you like and a syndicator you trust, many people will continue to build upon that relationship.

Tax Strategy

Every investor has different tax plans. Some are trying to avoid capital gains taxes—others are just looking to simplify their lives by filling out the easiest tax return possible! Depending on the structure of the opportunity, your level of involvement, and your tax advisor's knowledge, the tax implications of each deal will be very different. Indeed, active involvement and passive involvement from a tax standpoint mean some-

Keeping money active and working is what investing is really all about.

thing different from a securities standpoint. We suggest you discuss this with your professional advisor. Just be aware that not all tax advisors have the same level of know-how. Find advisors who are truly experienced in tax strategy and asset protection.

Team

As they say, no man is an island. Working together as business partners and brothers brought tremendous strength and support through the years—allowing us to leverage each other's strengths, and even take a break when we need it! While passive investing lends itself to delegating to a trustworthy team that will invest for you, active senior housing investment also requires a reliable and trustworthy team. Who's your team? If you don't have one yet, time to leverage one or create one of your own!

Investment Level

How much are you willing to invest? And does it make sense to invest it—all of it—right now? Passive investments like private placements can allow entry at just $25,000 in some cases. Active investing—even when borrowing from a bank or equity partner—can cost quite a bit more. Take a good hard look at your finances and determine how much investment makes sense for you right now.

Do Good AND Do Well!

It was our love for our mother and passion for improving the lives of other aging Americans that brought us here. Yes, it was first the business and investment opportunity. But, we quickly learned it's about doing business well . . . and doing it with heart.

A wise mentor of ours once told us that in order to succeed we must, "Learn to work *first* from your head and then your heart." Notice, he didn't say "work only from you head," he said, "work *first* from your head . . . " Yes, there does need to be "heart" in this world of senior housing. That's one aspect that makes this opportunity so exciting. Knowing that this surging age wave will change our society for decades, and that the

Silver Tsunami has created a tremendous new opportunity to *"do good AND do well"* . . . is certainly appealing to many of us.

Know Thyself . . .

By this point, you know what's best for you—either active or

Yes, there does need to be "heart" in this world of senior housing. That's one aspect that makes this opportunity so exciting.

passive investing, or perhaps a mix of both! Either way, we're here to help you take your next steps forward. We know you will be glad you did! And we can't wait to work with you on this journey.

Do Good AND Do Well!

Gene Guarino and Jim Guarino

Residential Assisted Living Academy is America's premier training and consulting organization for those interested in discovering how to become an Owner/Operator of RAL senior care homes.

Since 2014, RAL Academy has assisted thousands of investor/entrepreneurs by providing educational opportunities;

- RAL Immersion Learning Events
- RAL Online Training Systems
- RAL Live Seminars
- Podcasts, Radio Programs and TV Interviews.

Please visit **RALAcademy.com** for additional information or call **480-704-3065**

Gene Guarino, founder/CEO
Residential Assisted Living Academy

Gene Guarino is America's #1 educator and thought leader in the exploding senior housing sector of residential assisted living. He has presented hundreds of educational programs, lectures and seminars for tens of thousands of entrepreneurs and investors since 1990.